COLLECTIVE CHAOS

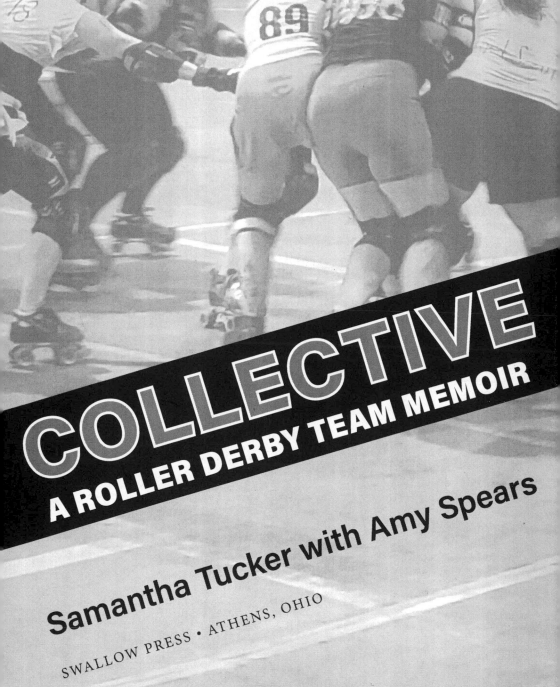

COLLECTIVE
A ROLLER DERBY TEAM MEMOIR

Samantha Tucker with Amy Spears

SWALLOW PRESS • ATHENS, OHIO

Swallow Press
An imprint of Ohio University Press, Athens, Ohio 45701
ohioswallow.com

To obtain permission to quote, reprint, or otherwise reproduce or distribute material from
Swallow Press / Ohio University Press publications, please contact our rights and permissions department at (740) 593-1154 or (740) 593-4536 (fax).

The opinions expressed herein are those of the authors and do not necessarily reflect those
of the publisher, Ohio University, or the State of Ohio.

Printed in the United States of America
Swallow Press / Ohio University Press books are printed on acid-free paper ∞ ™

30 29 28 27 26 25 24 23   5 4 3 2 1

Library of Congress Cataloging-in-Publication Data
Names: Tucker, Samantha, author. | Spears, Amy, 1976– author.
Title: Collective chaos : a roller derby team memoir / Samantha Tucker with Amy Spears.
Description: Athens : Ohio University Press, [2023]
Identifiers: LCCN 2022051202 (print) | LCCN 2022051203 (ebook) | ISBN 9780804012423
    (paperback) | ISBN 9780804041195 (pdf)
Subjects: LCSH: Tucker, Samantha. | Roller derby—Psychological aspects. | Self-actual-
    ization (Psychology) | Women roller skaters—Ohio—Biography. | Ohio—Biography.
Classification: LCC GV859.6 .T84 2023 (print) | LCC GV859.6 (ebook) | DDC 796.21092
    [B]—dc23/eng/20230109
LC record available at https://lccn.loc.gov/2022051202
LC ebook record available at https://lccn.loc.gov/2022051203

For Zee "Loraine Acid" Aria

Contents

Introduction

Roller derby operates in a space of both-and, never either-or. Skaters play offense and defense at once. The hits are as ferocious as the skate skills are precise. Roller derby is as rough as it is playful, as athletic as it is alternative, campy, and intense and beyond precise explanation. While the general public may (somewhat correctly) perceive our sport as ambiguous, the bigger issue is the general public's lack of perceiving us at all. Our full-contact sport on wheels is played by cis women, trans women, trans men, and nonbinary folks. And perhaps because sports fans aren't used to seeing a full-contact sport played by anyone other than cis men, people can't seem to get a grip on the nuanced, legitimate, refereed brutality of the modern, ever-evolving world of flat track roller derby.

Invented in 1935 by Chicago event promoter Leo Seltzer, the original Depression-era game was one of the first sports ever to feature men *and* women—teams were coed, but skaters alternated men on the track, then women. Eventually the sport moved to Hollywood through several 1950s roller derby movies and TV shows, and it gained international traction in the '70s with teams like the Tokyo Bombers. Roller derby was reinvented in every following decade, through the roller jamming of the '80s and '90s right up until the most modern version was established in the early 2000s, featuring the gender-expansive skaters we know and love today.

But as roller derby evolved into a revolutionary showcase of athletes largely ignored by the world of sports, the revolution remained on the roller derby track. US American culture has not run parallel and is, instead, on a track of devolution: Americans are busy supporting or churning out legislation to control other people's bodies, to ensure historically marginalized people stay in the margins. I'd argue that makes playing, even paying attention to a sport like roller derby, an act of subversion, of political defiance. Ours is now a sport with almost five hundred teams worldwide, played on every continent but Antarctica.

And yet—who is watching? Who is paying attention?

The following are questions we are frequently asked about the best sport if perhaps least understood sport in the world:

So, it's like a show, right? Is it a free-for-all? Can you punch people?

Is this WWE but with girls on wheels? Do you skate in lingerie?

And my personal favorite: Have you ever kicked someone in the face with a skate?

Queries like these might come from an innocent place and, I'm happy to say, seem less common than they once were. I, too, came to the best sport in the world with a misunderstanding of what was expected of me beyond fishnetted activewear and a clever, punny name. It is beyond measure, the pride I felt when I christened myself KEGEL SCOUT, #319. I admit, it makes sense, people asking the above kinds of questions of me, a person who spends at least 50 percent of her time choosing to be called by a word defined as a vaginal strengthening exercise.

Maybe the problem is mine. Maybe I enter these conversations defensively, the baggage of past conversations holding me down. For example, there was a beer festival I worked with Ohio Roller Derby, running coat check for cash tips, as our whole business operates on fundraising and dues and the invaluable volunteer efforts of league members. I passed out game schedule cards with coat check numbers and talked to people about derby. I took one man's coat, and when I returned his ticket to him, he said, "Well, I do love a woman who can take a hit."

We stared at each other. Where the hell does one go from there? The man turned a slight purple, mumbled an apology, and fled into the pretzels and froth. I wanted clarification. What was it that he truly meant to say? And how could we work together to frame it in a less domestic violence-y kind of way?

What I'm getting at is that telling people I play a brutal, body-breaking game, one that is both real and performative, where mostly cis women, and trans women, trans men, and nonbinary folks are the main play-ers (because there is roller derby, and *then* there is men's roller derby), well, for many, it's too much to fathom. It can't be allowed in all its com-plexity. It has to be whittled down to something accessible, palatable, for the audience that our culture, our world, still centers—cis White men. That assumed audience may identify what they define as sexy women hitting other sexy women. That audience has not often provided, has not *been* provided, opportunity to let women and trans people and gender-expansive and queer people define themselves, to play a sport made by and for themselves. I find the people involved in roller derby are often very grateful to finally have a people and place where they can joyfully take up space. A team of misfits can be a glorious thing, lucky too; ours is a choreographed chaos, one we can only manage together.

In the spirit of such collectivist complexity, we've decided to call this book a "Team Memoir," which mirrors the dual authorship of this book, and the player profiles we've written, with great love, featuring some of Ohio Roller Derby's most enduring players, those who are the reason we are still around, no matter if they still skate with us or not. We—Samantha Tucker, a.k.a. Kegel Scout, and Amy Spears, longtime leader and unofficial Ohio Roller Derby historian—had no choice but to build this narrative together. While my perspective is as an outsider coming into the fold, a cultural critic in search of community and com-monality, Amy has been involved with the world's fastest-growing sport since the near beginning. She has witnessed the accelerated growth, change, and evolution of this sport from a vantage point unavailable to most of today's players. She can attest to the ever-collective nature of this game and its international governing body. The sections titled "A Word from Amy Spears" remind us that the only way women's flat track roller derby survived, and evolved, was through the combined time, energy, and dedication of skaters, officials, volunteers, and fans—a group of people who pay to participate, co-operating and trying very hard to keep a legit but marginalized sport going, forever.

And here I am, always back at the same insistence that roller derby is a *real* sport. Whatever that means. It is festive in attire and punk rock in attitude and political by nature and athletic as fuck. It is a series of two-minute races between jammers, who are helped or hindered by blockers, blockers who play offense and defense at precisely the same time. Roller derby is a sport with beautifully complex rules and an international presence, and once our world championship game was played on ESPN. Well, it originally aired live on ESPN 2 but then it was bumped to ESPN 3 for reruns, replaced on the lower-numbered channel by live-action cornhole,[1] a sport of sorts, with a larger audience than the Women's Flat Track Derby Association. Or at least an assumed larger audience, per ESPN 2.

Through the course of this book you might learn how to play roller derby, or you may come to vaguely understand how *we* play roller derby. We hope you will come to love roller derby and admire the tenacity of a game that continues to succeed on the fringe, despite an American culture that allowed for its creation but fails to support its growth. We hope you cherish our teammates and opponents, our chosen family, as much as we do. But most importantly, we want you to know who is included in this family, this collective *we*, why *we've* continued to play, and how *we* cannot stop bettering what *we've* started, together.

---

1   Never heard of cornhole until Ohio.

The Basics

What the Heck Is Roller Derby Anyway?

Roller derby is a full-contact sport, played on roller skates. We call them "quads" after their four wheels, set in a square formation.

Our roller derby is on a flat track, played on a variety of surfaces. All you need is enough square footage to lay out an 88-foot-long oval of rope covered in gaffer tape. Add a couple of benches for teams and some folding chairs for a penalty box, and other than the players and officials, you're basically set.

The game moves counterclockwise around the track.

Skating officials, or refs, patrol from both the infield and a lane outside the track, calling penalties and counting points scored. Non-skating officials take care of duties such as running the clock, penalty box management, and tracking the score.

A game—also sometimes historically called a "bout"—is made up of two 30-minute halves, which are further divided into jams. A jam lasts for a maximum of two minutes, but can be even shorter depending on the strategies of the teams playing.

A team's game day roster consists of 15 skaters. Five from each team take the track at any given time, including the following players:

- One jammer: The jammer wears a star on their helmet and essentially *is* the ball, or scoring apparatus. (There is no ball in roller derby!) They must pass their opponents, with the help of their teammates, earning one point per opponent passed.
- One pivot: The pivot wears a stripe on their helmet and is a blocker with the special ability to become the jammer

for strategic purposes by "passing the star"—a move where the jammer gives them their helmet cover and also their position.

- Three blockers: As it sounds, they block. Both offensively (to get their jammer through) and defensively (to prevent the opposing jammer from passing). All at the same time.

Thirty seconds go onto the clock to give time for players to get into position. The jam timer calls out "Five seconds!" before blowing the whistle that starts the jam. Both jammers try to get through the pack of blockers, and the first one to get out front is declared "lead jammer," which gives them the power to decide when the point scoring and jam end. Both jammers can then score points on their second trip through the pack, earning one point per opposing blocker passed each lap. Jammers can use evasive skating like jukes and jumps, assistance from their own blockers, or they can power through by lowering a shoulder to push their opponents' walls forward.

At the end of two minutes, if the lead jammer hasn't already called it off, the officials blow four whistles to end the jam.

Thirty seconds elapse, the players line up, and a jam starts all over again. At the end of the game, the team with the most points wins.

While the game is full contact, it is *not* a free-for-all. Blockers can check opponents with the area between their shoulders and above their knees, but they cannot use forearms, hands, or elbows. No kicking allowed! Heads and spines are illegal hits, and it's also illegal to move opposing players backward. Blockers can skate the opposite direction on the track, but they can't hit anyone while doing so. Players who are knocked out of bounds can't return in front of people, but must reenter behind the player who knocked them out to avoid cutting the track. All blockers on both teams are responsible for making sure the pack stays together, and the game's action takes place within a range of 20 feet in front of or behind that pack. Anything outside all of these rules sends the offending player to the penalty box for 30 seconds.

That's a lot, but that's also what's in our heads constantly as we propel around the track, turning left, and left again.

All of that is the boring part, the nuts and bolts. But what roller derby actually is, is far more enthralling. There are leaps, spins, evasive maneuvers. There are huge hits, but also tiny, barely perceptible strategic movements that can have an outsize effect on the outcome of a game. A lot of people learn to roller skate casually without ever learning how to move sideways, skate backward, or even stop, but all of these are critical for roller derby players.

Roller derby is a great equalizer when it comes to athletes of all body types. There is no real advantage to inhabit a body of a particular size or shape, with the caveat that if all else is equal, it's probably the lowest center of gravity that ironically comes out on top.

When the whistle blows, you're in for up to two minutes of strategy, roller skating, athleticism, and passion. Because for many of us who play, it's gone beyond mere sport and into the realm of lifestyle. There's community and camaraderie, joy, sometimes tears, a little bit of blood, and a whole lot of sweat. Oh so much sweat.

And that's just the game itself. There's also all the preparation before that. The track setup, cross-training, marketing, fundraising. The double duty we do as athletes and business owners, while also trying to be a social good.

Roller derby is *not* a utopia. It's life changing for a lot of those involved, and like anything, sometimes the life changes aren't positive. People like to say that you get out of something what you put into it, but realists know that's not always true. Sometimes your effort outweighs the benefits you reap. Sometimes you put so much work into something that doesn't pan out. It doesn't mean it was all a waste. It doesn't mean you burn it to the ground, but we can't venerate everything we put our energies to.

Sometimes the game is fast, sometimes it's slow. It's usually exciting—even if a game is a blowout, someone's probably still doing great things, and then the fun in watching is finding and appreciating them.

That's the gist. It's strategic. It's powerful. It's played all over the planet. And the vast majority of roller derby, unlike most contact sports, is played by cis women, trans women, trans men, and nonbinary people.

1 These United Skates

Perhaps I've always been on my way to Ohio, even destined to be an Ohioan. When I first got here, I thought to myself, "What is Ohio? How? And also, why?" But now I've been here near a decade and I've figured some things out.

For instance, if the state of Ohio were in need of a catchphrase, I'd propose:

Ohio, the America of America.

When I say Ohio is the America of America, I'm trying to capture that loyal, averagely exceptional, self-made cultural spirit of Ohio—that is, so many Ohioans are content to recognize themselves as a people with a can-do attitude, despite tread-upon realities; here, we are ever bootstrapping and overcoming, just like Americans.

Just like America. Which may, in fact, be the Ohio of the world.

Unfortunately, the state of Ohio is not in need of a catchphrase. If anything, it already suffers too many. The current welcome signs at any Ohio state border proclaim *Ohio: Find It Here.* This imprecise slogan was launched in 2019 to replace the early 2000s' *Ohio, So Much to Discover.* Things were slightly less vague back in 1984—the year I was born in the square state of Colorado—when the Ohio Division of Tourism and Travel came up with *Ohio, the Heart of It All.* The reasoning behind this motto was both the location and a supposed heart-like shape of the state, though Ohio is no more a heart shape than Colorado is a triangle. In 1959, Ohioans mandated that *With God, All Things Are Possible.* It is unclear whether all these things are only possible in Ohio, and stop being so once in Indiana or West Virginia or Kentucky or that state up north, but I myself have uttered the phrase in the self-checkout line of an overrun Kroger, and I made it out alive. The oldest state slogan I found for this amorphous heart was made immediately after the Civil War; *Imperium in Inpeno,* Latin for "An Empire within an Empire," was decidedly too narcissistic and individualist, too self-indulgent and self-congratulatory, for a state within a union that was attempting to put itself back together. It lasted all of two years, 1865–67. Rest in Peace, meta-empiredom.

Based on the aforementioned history of why, where, and what Ohio is or does, I will confidently say *my* proposed slogan-motto-catchphrase is the most accurate, most succinct, most vaguely precise of them all. Ohio is an average place, or a place of averages. Ohio, the America of America nods to the state's enduring influence as a precise, local gauge of national political trends. It can refer to the surprising racial, economic, and cultural diversity of the Midwest state, which touts a population over 11,000,000—seventh largest in the country. It also works as a critique, offering up Ohio as a mirror of the best and worst of these United States: farmland, football, Indigenous history and Indigenous mockery, guns and fast-food testing grounds and university after university, people of every kind of community with their own take on all of it, their agreement only in that Ohio is the place to be—or it's where they are, in any case.

Before I arrived here, I'd long been overcoming my own American variety of obstacles and impostor syndromes, handed down to me by immigrant Korean and German grandmothers, enlisted grandfathers, my single mother, my addict father, my tenacious siblings. Ours has been the kind of difficult life movie stars and athletes like to shout out as the motivation for achieving greatness, the kind of struggle people brag about once they've found a way to move beyond it. I could not move beyond it fast enough, and in my determination, I fully expected a return of greatness. What I got was a decade of upheaval. This is the part of the story where a montage of agony presupposes a happy ending. Spoiler alert: movie stardom or championship levels of athleticism are not in my past, present, or future. Only Ohio.

But before Ohio: I graduated high school in 2002, and went to college in my home state, though three hundred miles from my hometown.

Naive idealist or great pretender that I am, I chose to use my full academic scholarship to study theater. My degree helped me act like my 20s were manageable. After graduation, I moved to New York City and planned to immediately star on *Saturday Night Live.* Instead, I worked three part-time jobs and when the cost of living grew higher than the limited satisfaction of struggling for my art, I moved back to Colorado in 2008. Upon my return, I lived a lifetime of years in two. My brother died. I married my college sweetheart. I tried my hand at this sport called roller derby. My body broke down, and without health insurance to support it. I worked four or five part-time jobs to get through the Great Recession.

I found no matter how many times I moved, it was never beyond struggle. In 2010, my new husband and I fled to South Korea because the American recession was simply too great. We found two years' worth of English teaching and happiness and health insurance and adventure, something like stability. But when 2012 hit, with our 30s coming in hot, we returned to Colorado, desperate to make America happen again.[1]

I'd been accepted for graduate school at Colorado State University, where I studied nonfiction so I could write about my family history and teach freshmen how to best communicate their own. I loved teaching and learning, and I wanted to make it my career. It wasn't until halfway through my time at CSU that I learned an MA in creative writing is not enough to gain tenured, full-time professorship, but instead, more part-time, uninsured, contractual work. I would need a terminal degree if I did not want to be stuck as an undervalued adjunct instructor, though even that would not guarantee an increasingly rare gig as a college professor. I needed to know people, make connections. I needed to publish, and publish more. My husband, an artist and bartender, was content to support me in any way he could. He was calm in the face of employment uncertainties, but one of us needed to get us both health insurance, and my career impulses had seemed the attainable route.

How could I ever self-actualize if I never got to be who I'd forever been trying to be, even if that person was just someone with financial, physical, mental stability? All I'd ever been told since I was a kid was that working hard, always trying, and going to school would ensure a living wage, a decent life. When I found out more school wasn't going to help me achieve stability in America, I defaulted to what I'd always

---

1   One does not make America; America makes you.

known. I would work harder, I would keep trying, and I would get *more* schooling. If one graduate degree was not enough to prove me worthy or employable, I would win another one.

Like Ohio, I've a deep need to be recognized as special despite perceived below-average beginnings, or a desire to appear special due to the hardships I've supposedly moved past. If an MA couldn't hack it, maybe a fully funded MFA would. Maybe more time to write and apply for grants would help cement the small successes I'd had as a writer, successes I worried may be flukes. I could not fathom that my need to be special, like everyone else, might never be realized, and in the ways I preferred. Ohio is America (is Ohio) because of this Rust Belt-y, not-quite-earned self-perception as the perennial underdog—an underdog who does well, even occasionally wins, who is shocked when they do, and bewildered when they find that winning is not enough to erase feeling like a loser.

I suppose I came to the state of Ohio in an Ohio-like state.

Upon my arrival in 2014, I was informed the school I'd attend for a second graduate degree was most accurately named THE Ohio State University. This certainly sounded like something special, though I had questions, like, Who was going to confuse OSU—over 60,000 students on 420 acres, a city unto itself—with any other university? Doesn't an entity insisting on articled clarification as the one and only, the singular . . . doesn't that beg mocking?[2]

I found Ohio as a place and a people as self-deprecating as they are proud, which describes me, in a buckeye[3] nutshell. In 2016, as I entered my third and final year at THE Ohio State University, I decided I might stay in Ohio a while. Otherwise proud Ohioans seemed to generally agree that moving to Ohio was suspect. They'd insist, *What are you doing here?* Ohioans are deeply loyal to Ohio, the America of America, but also confused by anyone who might go out of their way to end up here. I've experienced Ohioans listing every single president

---

2   At the genesis of my Ohio citizenry, my answer would have been an emphatic *yes*. Now I wonder if it's something to aspire to, or who I've been all along: a person with a *The* at the front of my name.

3   A poisonous nut. A tree seed. A chocolate peanut butter dessert. A terrifyingly limber school mascot.

or famous person born of the state (we all agree, Toni Morrison is the most important and exceptional Ohioan to date) before they ask me, *You chose to move here? From Colorado?* This, even after I'd acquired the exhaustive list of Very Important Ohioans, offered by people sporting "Ohio Against the World" T-shirts, as if there were a global conspiracy against a generally nice group of innocuous people.

Their disbelief, their own impostor syndrome, belies the truth of Ohio, and Columbus specifically: there is much to love in the capital city beyond affordability and averageness. There are street festivals and eclectic restaurants and an exploding brewery culture and a sick arts scene. Then there is, of course, the long list of (men's) sports to drool over. In Ohio, sports is religion, and sports culture bursts with under-dogged zealotry. Folks love pro-hockey's Blue Jackets, the Columbus Crew soccer team, and above all else, the Scarlet and Gray. In fact, the sports teams of Ohio may best capture the competitive, fanatical nature of the state and its citizenry. In the America of America, the Cleveland Browns never win, never come within reach of the Super Bowl, but their hapless fan numbers stubbornly grow; in the Midwest, "the Cavs" is not only how I affectionately refer to my lower leg muscles, but also how we refer to Cleveland's first professional sports team to win a championship in over 50 years. The Bengals recently made their first Super Bowl appearance in over 30 years. And then there's that whole Buckeye Nation. In Ohio, the America of America, there is always someone to root for.

During my time at Ohio State, I began to suspect I wasn't brilliant enough to be in grad school in the first place. My classmates had, as undergrads, attended Ivys, near-Ivys, and sub-Ivys before embarking on their own Midwest experience. No one had heard of my alma mater, Mesa State College,[4] mostly because I didn't tell anyone about it. My classmates called each other a cohort. They read my essays about familial poverty with wide eyes and little to no recognition. Their people were the kind of people who used *summer* as a verb, tourists who found Ohio and the middle of America charming—in an ironic way. "Being here is like being in an episode of *Roseanne*," someone once told me, which I somehow took personally. None of my cohort could be blamed for my insecurities but that doesn't mean I didn't try. When that failed to work, when I was faced with admitting they probably had their own struggles, I pivoted.

---

4   Mesa State College: It Was More Than I Expected!

I tried to remember, What was I undeniably good at? What was it I did well? Who was I other than a graduate school fake, an arbitrarily employed phony? In a fit of inspired distraction, I dragged my red writer chair to my office closet and reached up to the highest shelf, where I'd hidden my dusty Riedell roller skates.

I first ventured out on quads at around four years old, those sturdy leather boot skates with thick rubber front toe stops, lengthy laces, four wheels fixed two by two. Quads are built to flow, to provide a rolling, weaving stability. I admit, my family had a brief flirtation with blades in middle school, but this was largely because everyone hooked up with those lesser-wheels for a hot '90s second. As a kid, I associated in-line skates, blades, or ice skates with the middle and upper class, due to both cost and access. I always felt drawn to my perceived democracy of quads, emblematic of my neighborhood crew hopping cracked sidewalks on secondhand wheels, drawn to the idea that skating rink inequalities could be addressed by simply getting back up again.

My movement in roller skates always seemed less like a vehicle or mode of transportation and more like an extension of my body. Quads facilitated movement and speed I did not harness on my own wide, high-arched feet. I ran on my skates before I rolled. By six, I aimed to win my age group's speed skate minute, an activity offered at every session, like Downtown, or Hokey Pokey. If the DJ tried to skip right to preteen or teens, I'd wipe my sweaty, crimped bangs off my forehead and shout at the booth. I'd raise my fist and insist on skating fast even if I was *the only* under-ten braving the slick. The disco ball, quarter lockers, arcade games, occasional laser tag, trashy snack bars—it all felt like home and set the scene for a healthy chunk of my childhood. Skating was never a sport to me, but a skill that came as naturally as breathing. This was how I preferred all I attempted in life: difficult for many, easy (in appearance) for me.

Maybe I was too dumb for this (elitist, probably) MFA degree, but I've always known I am brilliant at roller skating. I was in need of tangible validation. Dear, average, just right Columbus provided. Two rinks, in fact, both part of the serendipitously named chain, these United Skates of America.

I pledged immediate allegiance. Drowning in shame and self-doubt, I used my skates as a life preserver. At the rink I could avoid academia and pretentious people who use the term *academia,* even as I'd been brandishing the word like a parade baton days prior. I searched for a more familiar me at the United Skates of America, and there I was: under the strobe and the disco ball, glittering tassels dangling from ceiling tiles. Prince crooned "I Would Die 4 U" from the DJ booth speakers as I followed the confident swirl of bodies. Skaters smiled at me, a few White tattooed women who had the rockabilly look of roller derby. My Riedells, still laced with black and white, adorned with yellow leather toe guards, looked deceptively brand new. The black, white, yellow—these were the colors of the roller derby team I'd made in Colorado in 2010, a team I spent a sad total of three months on just after my brother died. Skating well did not equate to playing roller derby well.

I'd joined and quit the Pikes Peak Roller Derby in another anxiety-fueled, confusing, and sorrowful period of my life, that grief-riddled Colorado layover in between New York City and South Korea. Before Ohio, I associated the skates with one of the worst periods of my life. My expensive, top-of-the-line quads were a reminder of great pain, extreme life changes, and a shameful attempt at athleticism. Here I was, strapped back in for more rolling distraction. I find when people, even entire states, feel insignificant and lost, they begin throwing out the most arbitrary life preservers. For example, when Ohio adopted its state flag in 1902, it had already been a state for 100 years, had long since earned its moniker as "Mother of Presidents." This longevity, this record of leadership, was not enough for Ohio's ego. It was time to make a state flag unlike any other, the only state flag not rectangular in shape, but triangular, like a pennant![5]

In reality, my reclamation of skating was not arbitrary, not some weird-shaped flag as a cry for help. It was home. When I was younger, before I knew to be ashamed of my family's lack, the Academy Boulevard Skate City of Colorado Springs was a place anyone could find flow. There was always something egalitarian about my happy place, a pulsing Day-Glo rave on wheels, rogue, inexpensive childcare for parents, a place for poor kids, middle-class kids, and even the poor kids'

---

5   A Word from Amy Spears: Ahem. It's a *burgee.* A double-pointed pennant, unique among state flags. And we love it.

rich cousins. Skaters were Black, White, Korean, Japanese, Mexican, Puerto Rican, many ethnicities, all ages, great in our cultural differences and brought together by our love of roller skating.

Adult nights at the Columbus United Skates were no different, though the skill levels far exceeded the stumbling I remembered as a kid. Here, there were a handful of White skaters. Most kept falling down and appeared to be on terribly inept first dates. The majority of skaters in Columbus are Black. At Adult Night, 18-year-olds jammed on skates, landed handstands and high jumps, then 60-year-olds arrived and did much of the same. As folks led pulsing line dances, I sped in and out of all at high speeds, sweaty but smiling, lost in movement instead of my mind. I got caught up in the '90s R&B, the smell of popcorn and sweat and old carpet, the optimistic shine of the skate floor. Roller skaters are my people, a we of sharp denim jeans and bright leggings, baggy band shirts or self-made crop tops, gilded fanny packs, and folded handkerchiefs to mop our collective forehead sheen. We pulsed to the beat, separate but together.

A fleeting, foolish series of thought: If the state of Ohio could go to great lengths to prove it was worthy, relevant, I could, too. Sure, I had a graduate thesis to write and defend, hundreds of theoretical pages to read a week, undergraduate papers to grade. Anxiety and writer's block insisted there was no better way to finish my degree than by rolling on as if it were already done. Perhaps it was time for a comeback. A quick Google search would tell me if Ohio had a women's flat track roller derby team, and maybe tryouts—

The idea alone made my back seize, my knees cry out, "You stupid bitch!"

I took a break in the snack bar, filled my water bottle at the incompetent water fountain, and reconsidered my reconsideration. I felt relief in my skates, my mental gymnastics dulled by how fully I dropped into my own body, into physicality and flow. Why would I undermine this reunion with myself with another inevitable failed attempt at sports and athletics?

The rink was joyful and absent the exhaustive posturing of higher education. I was looking to simplify, not complicate. This rink is where I belonged, not in a stuffy classroom with people who knew canon to be important books by important White men rather than the homonym that goes boom.

Candace "Chainsaw" Moser Stafford
(Credit: Candace Moser Stafford)

OHIO PLAYER PROFILE: THE TINY DICTATOR

I always hear Chainsaw before I see her, guttural cackles and staccato shrieks announcing her arrival. When she is excited, her sentences raise in volume, pitch, tempo, not unlike the way an actual chainsaw winds up, then growls out. A lot of her sentences end like this. Her sound is extroverted, and people come to know her by this projected loudness, but Chainsaw keeps her circle tight and her energy local, and she often can't be bothered with clunky niceties. This is not personal or mean, and later, Chainsaw will say as much. It's just—Chainsaw has no time to suffer fools. She is our current and longest-serving executive director. Chainsaw is keeping the league together. Chainsaw is making everything better.

Chainsaw is very small in stature, but in style and outward confidence and roller derby expertise and eclectic talents and jobs and league management, she is probably 8'5". On the karaoke stage, she is 10 feet tall. She'll sing "O Holy Night" at midnight in July, nostalgic for her Catholic family, and then she'll get up early the next morning to teach her daughter's Girl Scout troop how to roller skate, or do archery, or build fires.

Chainsaw has broken everything, including her back. She had to have back surgery, and there are bolts on her spine, and two incision scars, one front, one behind. Chainsaw is one of the best skaters Ohio, and likely the sport of roller derby, will ever see. Chainsaw can't stop skating, even as Chainsaw is in chronic pain.

Blockers often get overlooked because their job is less obvious than jamming, less dazzling, but when Chainsaw blocks, I see nothing else. Which is wild, because she is hard to see; she is so slight, which makes it ever more satisfying when she's ruining the other team's life, when she sticks to players like, well, *like a fly on shit,* as Chainsaw might describe it. On Derby Twitter she is referred to as "Lil' Naked 19" because she blocks in her cropped jersey and hot pants (with a french fry fabric, bet she made them herself) because Chainsaw prizes comfort above all else and it's stifling in most of these warehouse situations we play in and—ope,[6] the other jammer had no idea they came *not* to play but to get knocked out of bounds and drawn way the fuck back, on the track, by Chainsaw.

Again.

And again.

How can I even begin to describe a draw-back by Chainsaw? It would best be shown in GIF form, and Chainsaw is working on all the training GIFs right now. She is watching playoffs and champs with the kind of scrutiny and discernment one gives the thing they are an expert in. This is how they became an expert in it. Chainsaw grew up at the skating rink like many of us did, another poor kid, a misfit in a family of misfits, the oldest kid taking care of everyone else, a leader by default, which is how the best leaders are made.

Chainsaw designs and creates incredible activist jewelry. She sells earrings at punk rock flea markets that say NOT WITHOUT A WARRANT and TERFS NOT WELCOME and MEN ARE TRASH. Chainsaw has the kind of alternative style I coveted but failed to produce, for many years, this DIY, Rockabilly Punk/Goth/Cosplay brilliance, all perfect black bangs and electric-blue highlights. She is effortlessly cool. Her husband, St. Drewcifer, will agree, even if she does not.

If there is anything Chainsaw can't do, then Drewcifer has got it covered.

When she is not homeschooling her most-excellent child, or volunteering at any given place, taking beautiful photos, or rebuilding every single poorly assembled skate on our team, she is also league president. She leads with a Mexi-Coke in one hand and a rotisserie chicken in the other. These are all she ever asks for in return. They are her currency; it is the very least we could pay her.

—Kegel Scout

---

6   *Ope* is Midwestern for "Excuse me."

A Word from Amy Spears, Ohio Native

I've never had any great sense of Ohio pride, despite having never lived anywhere else. Or maybe because of that fact. It's not like I chose Ohio; I just started my existence here. I intended to leave at some point and never got around to it. Circumstances never lined up properly, and at some point, inertia took over.

I grew up in rural southwestern Ohio, a place so un-notable that even people from Ohio are like, "Wait, what's in southwestern Ohio?" The answer to that is not the name of a city or other attraction, but flat farmland. Corn and soybeans and hogs and cattle.

Our school was small and rural enough that field trips required travel, whether to a nearby skating rink or further to the air and space museum in Dayton or to Columbus for the zoo or the Ohio History Connection and its associated replica pioneer town (ever-so-descriptively named Ohio Village). We would pack sack lunches, board a big yellow school bus, and make a long drive to view the Ice Age–era mastodon skeleton.

Never in a million years did I think that three decades later, as an adult, I would be in a photo on display in the museum within yards of that mastodon. And especially not as the result of being included in an exhibition about Ohio sports.

My entire sporting history pre-roller derby consisted of summer Little League baseball and tee-ball until I was about 10, and a very short stint of hurdles[7] in junior high track. After that, I didn't even try to enjoy the sports-centric culture (specifically football) of my small town. To the contrary, I spent my time as field commander of my high school marching band, only barely grasping how the scoring in football worked enough to know when to start the school fight song from the stands.

In 2018, the Ohio History Connection contacted Ohio Roller Derby about their upcoming exhibition on sports in Ohio history. We had recently, in the interest of better reflecting the identity of our

---

7   This should have been an early sign of what types of sports I would actually enjoy. It's not enough for me to play a sport that involves running back and forth—no, I require wheels strapped to my feet. So running in a straight line? How about let's add some obstacles to that, so then it seems worth doing?

membership, changed from our original name of Ohio Roller Girls to Ohio Roller Derby. As such, Burnadeath—our league executive director at the time—had commissioned a new version of our team flag to reflect our new acronym of OHRD, rather than OHRG. At our end-of-year awards banquet that year, Burna presented the new flag as I told the story of the birth of our original flag for those who were too new to yet know it. We decided to donate that original flag to the museum for the exhibit, as a way of marking the moment in our own history, and the importance of recognizing how sports are changing, in how they are affected by gender as well.

Burna and I did a video interview with the staff of the museum, sitting down to talk about the history of our sport and the history of our league. I talked about the origin of our team flag during our second season. It had been commissioned by our original team coaches shortly in advance of our first tournament appearance, sewn by a skater's grandmother, and first flown as a surprise to our players during our intros at that tournament. It's Kelly green and black—our team colors—but otherwise a faithful copy of the stripes on the flag of the state of Ohio, a double-pointed pennant called a burgee. The red circle in the center is replaced by a jammer star, one of a total of 14 stars on the flag, representing the number of skaters on a game day roster.[8]

And presently, that flag resides—along with our team photo—in the entrance to the museum, making it hard for me not to identify as an Ohioan, or an Ohio athlete.[9]

I've skipped over so much, though, so let me explain how I ended up in this improbable situation.

---

8   The roster capacity became 15 as a result of a later Women's Flat Track Derby Association rules change, so we probably need to sew on another star.

9   I will never in my life forget the first time someone referred to me as an athlete. It was one of those two early coaches, Tank, who also doubled as an announcer. He was practicing announcing in preparation for a game while we were skating laps, doing play-by-play at the rink. I approached a corner and started my crossovers to pick up speed and overheard him say, "And here comes Alli Catraz, a natural athlete." I laughed so hard at this I nearly fell off my skates, and he was very confused by my reaction.

Those in the thick of roller derby can easily list the worst of the general public's questions: Where's the ball? Do you have to be gay/butch/big/punk/tattooed/et cetera? What does your family say? Do you get to throw elbows? Better than therapy, eh? And my all-time *not* favorite question: Do you skate naked? What spurs someone to ask this? Who would even want to see that? Someone once told me there was a YouTube video of some Canadian men playing ice hockey naked—and yes, at this point in our pop culture cred, there are even derby porn films in existence—but for the love of God people, let's think critically for half a second about how you would feel if I answered yes before you ask me something like that. (Could there be a better example of *Seinfeld*'s "bad naked"?)

Another of my least favorites is "How did you get involved in roller derby?" Not so much because it's an annoying question or difficult for me to answer, but because I don't know what the asker really wants to know. I'm not sure they know either, or if they are even asking the right question. Do they mean "How did you get involved?" or do they mean something more like "Why on earth do you, as a grown-ass, apparently functional adult, spend six hours a week with wheels strapped to your feet hitting other adults?"

"How" is definitely not what they want to hear. They don't want to know about how we have to be able to skate 27 laps in under five minutes or the minutiae of the process between seeing a flyer in a bar, and actually realizing the goal of purposefully running into your new friends while roller skating circles in front of a crowd. They don't want whatever surprisingly mundane story exists of how anyone actually gets into roller derby. No, they expect some exotic story, as if I've run away with the circus or joined a cult.

Which, in some ways, one could argue, I have.

So, what I usually draw on is my own skating history. The sheer joy of skating, the rare school trips to the United Skates of America outpost in nearby Springfield, Ohio. My family still has an 8mm film reel from the day my dad stopped at a garage sale on his home from town with two pairs of pristine, leather-booted roller skates for which he had paid a nickel each. That price seems preposterous, but this was the early 1980s. (The 1900s! The prior millennium!) In the jerky, grainy footage, I am walking up the concrete porch stairs of our farmhouse wearing a sundress, with said skates on my feet, three sizes too big, laced up to my knees, with what I thought were dainty Dorothy Hamill–esque arm movements. And with pinkies up, which is how I am still photographed, even in the toughest of games.

If I try to watch it now, it jumps all around since we don't have a workable projector, but you can still tell that in that moment, I am *thrilled*. I prance around on bearingless, half-inch-wide metal wheels.[10] It looks terrifyingly dangerous, but in that rare footage, in true little kid fashion, I am unfazed.

And sometimes I'll mention that I grew up watching *RollerJam* on TV in the 1990s. I was in junior high, and there were hair metal bands on the show at halftime, and that was my thing. I would set our VCR to record after *Friday Night Videos,* and then Saturday morning get up and watch women with huge coifs fake wrestle each other on roller skates near an alligator pit.

It was absurd. I loved it.

Those are the loose, appropriate-for-flyering-in-a-park reasons why I joined derby. They're the undercurrent of why this seemed like a good idea—or even a possibility—once the opportunity arose. But there's so much more.

I remember exactly where I was when I came across the Texas Rollergirls in a blurb in *Bust* magazine: sitting at the counter near the back patio in the lunchroom at my boring job.

I remember it so clearly for two reasons. One, I was interrupted by one of my coworkers stopping to say hi. All of the programmer dudes I worked with seemed to find it odd that I chose to eat lunch with a book, apart from them, and they seemed to want to take pity on me because of this. In reality, I desperately needed a break from spending every minute of my workday with them, and this exacerbated the issue further. Two, I can remember the excitement in my gut that sat there waiting as I finished exchanging vague pleasantries with the brogrammer because it's what made me think that this was An Important Blurb in that magazine.

This was probably around 2004. This revival of roller derby had started back up in Austin, Texas, in 2001, but the internet and social media were still young enough that word didn't travel that fast, and so it hadn't reached me that this was happening. It was the pre-viral age, if you will.

---

10   As an adult, I learned these "wheels" were actually airplane bearings, engineered for flight.

Between 2001, when Texas Rollergirls and Texas Roller Derby started up,[11] and 2006, when I finally walked in the door to what was then named the Ohio Roller Girls, the growth of derby moved in a slow and steady line—with the emphasis on slow. Many of the early teams who formed in the years just after Texas existed because someone had a sister away at college, or a friend came to visit and then went home and started a team of their own. It was a very organic growth, based on word of mouth. If it was on the internet at all, it was on Myspace. Texas released a DVD of games, and that was passed around and studied. Many teams who began in that era have a similar story: one or two interested folks put out a call by posting flyers in bars and cafés, and if they were tech savvy, maybe Craigslist or local listservs. Then a meeting was held of interested people (also usually in a bar), followed by an awkward meetup at a local skating rink where everyone tried to remember the skills they'd honed as children in dusty rental skates. Those people were usually women recently out of college, or of that age, grunge and punk and emo looking.

In the case of Ohio, our first meeting took place at a bar and pizza shop north of Ohio State University's campus. It was April 23, 2005, and the people who showed up were mostly young women in their early 20s. I knew about it, I did not go, and while part of me is sad I wasn't present on day one, I also don't think I would have made it through to the first game if I had been, due to how my own life went over that summer. I was on the Yahoo! group, having found a flyer in a bar advertising the meeting. I had a weirdly voyeuristic lurker role in seeing a lot of what went down in the early days.

Scarlette Fury, the main founder, was a recent college graduate, and she'd had some contact with people who were in teams across the country. She also had a great organizational streak and pushed those early members to create (or steal)[12] policies. The group chose and eventually

---

11 While I do know folks who were there, I was half the country away and my information is secondhand at best. The great *Rollergirls: True Tales from the Track,* by Melissa "Melicious" Joulwan, contains this story in great detail, as told by someone who lived it.

12 Is it stealing if it's with permission? Those early years were filled with emails full of policy docs, track diagrams, and rules drafts, freely shared from team to team. That collaborative spirit is the undercurrent that still runs through the sport and the Women's Flat Track Derby Association.

abandoned the original name (Capital City Rollers) and colors (lime and teal because that was the stock shirt CafePress had available). They rented time at the local skating rinks after they closed for the evening and set up a regular 9:00 p.m. to 11:00 p.m. practice schedule. To pay for it, they charged dues and raised funds with bands playing shows and staging full-contact musical chairs events. And they promoted tirelessly, with a relentless word-of-mouth campaign to drum up excitement about the first game (scheduled a year to the day after that first meeting) and to recruit skaters.

I knew about all of this and was following along on the Yahoo! group. I didn't read everything, but I popped in from time to time to nose around and see if I felt like I could bring myself to show up. The fact that I hadn't joined yet was not only because I am a naturally shy person, but because my shyness was compounded by being in the middle of one of the worst years of my life.

There are a lot of people's derby stories that begin this way—things fell apart, and then I tried roller derby. As if the sport existed to take us back to a time before our trauma, the joy of strapping wheels to our feet transporting us back to childhood. Transporting me back into my family's eerily silent 8mm footage, gliding around carefree.

2 Small to Get Big

Back at grad school, I steered all conversations to roller skating. I did not want to acknowledge my intellectual insecurities, and I wanted a break from the national political nightmare that was 2016, or really the entire history of this country, so I did not hesitate to brag, at length, about the speed and skill I still possessed. I also had no problem referencing my (90 days) time as a roller derby player in Colorado, though I kept the specifics to myself. I could not see the harm in letting peers believe I was strong and fearless enough to play a sport as perilous as derby. If it distracted them from seeing me as an intellectual fraud, or allowed me temporary reprieve from wallowing in despair at the rise of all-American fascism, then so be it. I directed people in my cohort to social media, to pictures proving my time served as a roller derby team member. I hoped others grazed my Facebook photo album, creatively titled "Roller Derby," and encountered a recklessly cool badass, me in full gear, making tough expressions on the track, surrounded by teammates I could hardly remember.

If anyone looked too closely, they'd see past to who I actually was half a decade prior: a grief-stricken, lost 25-year-old, afraid of adulthood and life, which was, at closer examination, also a fear of death. Death was the real impetus of the whole lark. My brother died, I joined a roller derby team. I had spent most of the years since trying to forget. I left these details out of my academia-avoidant conversations, tried to keep Monday copy machine chats upbeat:

"How was your weekend?"

"Oh, it was great. I went roller skating because it's the only way I can keep from completely loathing myself."

It was after another Sunday night session at the U. Skates of A. when a professor overheard me skate-bragging. This same professor had recently called me to his office to discuss my general classroom demeanor. He said he'd never met someone with such "cheerful disdain," even as he accepted, without comment, the same criticisms I offered from even more abrupt male classmates. This so-called professor and I shared a gasoline-and-matches kind of chemistry, which is to say he found his pedagogy illuminating and I was like, *I'll show you illuminating.*

Our exchange was familiar. I learned at an early age that boys were not huge fans of me. I was not agreeable and I was bossy. This might also be phrased as "interested in leadership" or "vocally motivated" or "a girl who is unable to be quiet," but in any case, it made middle school me the easiest target for a large group of competitive, mediocre boys. Sometimes those boys grow into men like this professor. The professor and I did not do well at hiding our mutual distaste and instead avoided each other, so I was surprised to find him standing behind me at the English department copier as I continued letting my peers believe I was a grizzled veteran roller derby player.

"You played roller derby?" If he had been standing any closer to the conversation, he might have gotten slapped in the face when I undoubtedly flipped my hair over my shoulder.

"Yes," I answered, weary. "Why?"

"Do you know Amy Spears?"

The name sounded familiar, but I couldn't place it. I shook my head, considered excusing myself to the bathroom, but the professor continued.

"Yeah, Amy Spears works in this department. Her office is on the third floor."

Sigh. Everyone knows someone who saw someone say they played roller derby. "No, can't say that I know her," I said.

"Well, she played roller derby."

"Ah! Do you know her derby name? I might know her by that." I wouldn't.

"I'm pretty sure she went by Amy Spears. She played with Ohio for a long time, but she retired."

"Really? That's cool." Great. Now I'd have to stop telling people I'd done a thing I'd barely even done because someone else in close proximity had actually, truly done it.

"Yeah—I'm surprised you haven't met her. Amy Spears. They say she's famous in roller derby." Looking back, I'm sure he must have—for once—been making innocent conversation. I remember this talk, that went on far too long, longer than any we've had since, and in that season of martyrdom, I saw his interjection, his admission of the words *Amy Spears,* as sabotage.

This dude had found me out. I did not belong in grad school, in the state of Ohio, or on skates. I excused myself to the bathroom.

I was about to be exposed A Fraud, a roller derby fraud, a forever Fresh Meat who didn't even hack it for three months, a wannabe who got hurt *rurl* bad and quit but still bragged about being a supposed roller derby player to classmates for masturbatory reasons whilst I happened to be standing on the floor above someone with such an already excellent legal name she used it for her derby name, a person who played for *Ohio,* one of the best teams in the country.

Later, at home in my red writer chair, my Riedell skates on the floor beside my desk, I Googled "Amy Spears roller derby" and "Amy Spears WFTDA." And there she was: a skater who started with Ohio the very year the league formed, 2006; Amy Spears, former president of the league and recurrent board member; Amy Spears, namesake of Ohio Roller Derby's Amy Spears Award; Amy Spears YouTube family interview at Ohio's 2012 playoffs; Amy Spears, team captain; Amy Spears, July 2015 WFTDA Featured Skater.

The last thing I remember before I blacked out was Amy Spears: elected vice president of the international Women's Flat Track Roller Derby Association in 2015.

The cultural attitude, the very American-ness of Ohio, our Little America, is present in a bowl of Cincinnati chili, in the cocoa and cinnamon-spiked lump of hot brown sandwiched between a nest of spaghetti and four fistfuls of fresh grated cheddar. Upon my first meeting with this dish, I asked, But why?

To which Ohioans, our dear Ohio Americans, would surely reply, "Why not?"

In this metaphor, I believe I'm suggesting a second shot at roller derby as the exotic and dangerous chili. Or perhaps the chili is my impostor syndrome, and while I'm asking why, maybe Amy Spears is the genial, casually supportive Ohio American asking me, "Why not?"

I avoided Amy Spears for as long as I could. First, I pretended she didn't exist. Then I started peeking around her office on the third floor of the English department, where she managed the entire Digital Media Project. I heard her laugh as I lurked outside, and it sounded like the hearty laugh of a very well-adjusted person. It was the laugh that encouraged me to knock on her door and get this shit over with. "Hi! Amy Spears?"

The woman behind the desk smiled. She wore extremely clever tortoiseshell glasses and had knitting tattoos across her chest, the yarn and needles faintly visible above her T-shirt and cardigan. Her whole look said crafty, interesting—she was a person comfortable in her own skin, someone I liked immediately. I knew she'd be great; I didn't want to out myself as the great pretender.

"Yeah, that's me," she said, and smiled.

This was the only prompt I needed. I rambled on in a way that was reminiscent of telling on myself. This was something I did as a perfectionist little kid: run to my mother to tell on whatever small, insignificant sin I'd committed, in order to get ahead of probable punishment.

Before I told Amy of my roller derby failures and fraudulence, I made excuses: *Do you remember how wild the game was then, in 2010? Do you remember how dangerous?* And I didn't wait for answers because I was warming up on confessing all to Amy Spears, a stranger. I can't remember most specifics of our chat that day—and it was short, if excruciating for me—but I'm sure I spoke in one full block paragraph, perhaps a run-on sentence, at this person I had Googled extensively. It may have sounded something like this:

> Yeah, so my brother was killed in Iraq and that's why I started roller skating again in 2010 and suddenly that turned into trying out for roller derby. Do you know Pikes Peak Roller Derby? It's a team in Colorado, that's where I'm from, but I messed up my knee and then somehow, in my first bout, I broke my back—I didn't have health insurance, and wasn't even aware I had broken it until I moved here to Ohio in 2014, because, like I said, I didn't have health insurance, can you believe I skated without health insurance? I did it because, like I casually mentioned, my brother was killed in Iraq, then I broke my back, then I tried to walk it off, and it was all kind of a disaster.
>
> So, is it true that you are roller derby famous?

Amy Spears, longtime captain and excellent teammate and forever very good person, laughed, nodded, and shrugged. I don't believe I even told her my name, legal or otherwise.

Tarah "Bigg Rigg" Briggs
(Credit: Rachel Turner)

OHIO PLAYER PROFILE: THE HUMBLY GREAT

We call her Baby Jesus when once a year we split up into two teams, the Roller Ghouls and Jingle Bells, for our annual fundraiser game, the Skatemare Before Christmas. Rigg's stature (ironically not "Bigg"), and the fact that the Jingle Bells team proposed a play in which another player would actually physically carry her through the pack like an infant (swaddling optional), contributed to this moniker. The play never happened. The name stuck.

And so, Our Lord and Savior does not want to be named as such, but here she is, the love of our lives, our inspiration, Bigg Rigg. When Bigg Rigg reads this, she will shake her head at such proclamations, which only affirms her humble greatness.

Bigg Rigg is neither big nor rigged, which is obviously a part of the appeal—her athletic prowess is shocking, her gentle modesty astounding. She is smol and swol. She is doing more pullups than everyone else at the State Fair military recruitment table because she can. She is jumping four feet in the air, on skates, she is self-effacing even as she is flying. She is taking advantage of pandemic-induced free time to learn how to do a backflip, wearing a gray hoodie and gray sweatpants like they are the coolest attire you've ever seen.

Bigg Rigg is quiet, funny, the Whitest woman who knows every rap lyric on the hip-hop BBQ playlist.

Bigg Rigg is also one of the hardest workers I know—dedicated, driven, motivated, but in a very grounded, accessible way.

Unpretentious and patient as a trainer, she intuits minor tweaks to improve skating skill. She came to roller derby without an extensive history of athleticism, as most of us do, and still inhabits her body with the physical intelligence of a natural sportsperson. I have seen Bigg Rigg make moves that force gasps from the crowd, watched her glide through two packs of hulking blockers, then backbend, Matrix-like, as her single gloved hand slides out of bounds. In seconds she bends, supports her arched body, keeps her skates in play, then pops back up and hauls ass around the track. When Bigg Rigg returns to the bench, she is satisfied rather than celebratory, which helps remind us (me) we are all here to play together, not just fangirl over each other.

A physical therapist, Bigg Rigg is often the team's default medical aid at practice. These are the other moments that rob breath from a crowd, when downed skaters don't get back up. In moments like this, where the pain is electric and infinite, when the extent of an injury is undetermined but the fear of possibilities limitless, the immediate need is compassionate competence. And so Bigg Rigg arrives, leans over a shattered ankle, asks calm questions, helps a skater stay focused, brave.

Lara del Rage and I have what we call BRM, or Bigg Rigg Motivation. It's a hybrid of awe and guilt, a catalyst for playing better, faster, stronger. So many of us came to derby without any notion of being on a team, any understanding of what a full-contact, physically brutal sport demands. In derby, I've found it easier to believe that I am, will always be, somewhat of a joke on the track. Bigg Rigg has taught me to not fear taking myself seriously. This looks like coming to as many practices as possible, working out off-skates on my own time, studying tape, and not quitting when I am reminded that I can be somewhat of a joke on the track. Except I guess I'm not. Teammates often remind me there aren't a lot of people up for the task of roller derby.

Before a game, Bigg Rigg sits in the locker room with her headphones on. She wears a black Ohio Roller Derby hoodie and pulls the front down over her eyes so only her nose and mouth are visible. She looks like a Jedi, peaceful and centered. We will do anything in our power to make her proud; she makes us proud all the time. At a recent practice, for example:

"Hey, Kegel! You like Wendy's?"

"Yeah, Rigg, I like Wendy's."

"How about WHEN DEEZ nuts are on your face?"

Celebrities. They're just like us.

—Kegel Scout

A Word from Amy Spears, Slightly Famous in Roller Derby

In the beginning, way back in 2005, to become a skater with what was then called the Ohio Roller Girls, you had to do the following:

- Observe one practice.
- Start skating at practices (usually on those horrible brown rentals until you were able to buy your own gear online and have it shipped).
- Successfully complete four falling drills (roughly eight minutes total of falling down and getting back up again).
- Scrimmage at least twice. (This presumes at some point you read—and absorbed—the rules.)
- Get drafted to one of the four home teams.

That was it. I can feel our more recent rookie classes hating me a little as they spend anywhere from 6 to 18 months slogging away at practice before they ever see gameplay. But also, in just a month or two, most of them are already *far* better players than any of us in those early years could even dream of anyone being. And the roller derby part is a heck of a lot more sophisticated than the "skate fast, turn left" of our initial seasons.

At the time, depending on how well you could skate beforehand, this process could take anywhere from a few weeks to a year. In my case, I observed my first practice on January 17, 2006. I had my skates in my hand by January 27, had my falling drills done at the next two practices, and scrimmaged in early February. I was immediately put into the next team draft, and then I played at our first-ever game on April 23. A whopping three months from whim to skating in front of several hundred people who'd paid to see it.

Before joining, I'd seen flyers in bars for months and kept putting "send email to roller derby team" on my to-do list, then ignoring it. Eventually, I ran into a friend from high school and she mentioned she was playing roller derby in Columbus and that I should join. I told her I wanted to, but I didn't think I could. That I was so busy—or whatever excuse I made up for myself.

In truth, 2005 utterly broke me. I'd landed a job that should have been my dream job, but it was not exactly living up to what was promised—I needed that win, as my past job featured one of the worst bosses I've had to this day. One of my closest friends began struggling with substance issues right as I found out I had a rare condition that meant my ovaries had shut down. I was thrown into menopause at the age of 29. And then, in June, my ex-boyfriend Todd suddenly died with no warning. Todd was someone I'd met during college, at the Denny's my friend Dorothy and I hung out at after late nights editing for our film classes. A few years after I graduated, Todd and I found each other again, and we dated for a short time. It fizzled, but we remained close friends. One week we went to see Neko Case play at Little Brother's together, and the next, Todd's best friend was calling to tell me he was gone.

I was in an emotional tailspin and honestly, in retrospect, a pretty deep depression. I spent months stewing in my thoughts and doing not a lot more than simply existing before I decided to hit a reset button. I left my apartment, and my neighborhood, which both felt like they had too many ghosts at that point, and moved in with a friend across town. I started being able to go out again. I started a knitting group at a coffee shop/bar and made crafty friends. Slowly, I crept back into my own life. Or maybe I started figuring out what my life should be.

One night at Surly Girl, a now defunct Old West and pinup-themed bar, I ran into Foxy Force. Well, in my brain, she wasn't Foxy yet. She was still Alyssa, who I'd gone to high school (and middle school, and grade school) with and been in the same 4-H group with in our small farm town. She once again encouraged me to sign up for roller derby. In casual conversation, her then boyfriend and I somehow stumbled onto the realization that Todd was the first person he'd met when he moved to Columbus. I don't believe in things like signs, but I'd already felt like Todd's ghost was following me the whole summer anyway, so this felt like him pushing me forward. I made a New Year's resolution to finally join roller derby.

Then, knowing myself all too well, I made a second resolution: roller derby would be a thing that I would do for fun, and not a thing I would end up in charge of, like most endeavors in my life. It would be an outlet, not a stressor. I later told a college friend all this, and his response was to simply laugh at me. Because he knew how I am, how this would end up, even if I wouldn't admit it.

Coming in at the beginning, I didn't quite realize that we were still inventing the sport of roller derby. Having seen that blurb in *Bust* magazine made it feel like this was a thing that existed, whole and fin-ished. But it was still so very malleable. And since most roller derby leagues (and the WFTDA) were and are collectively managed and democratically run, everyone gets their hands dirty in the running of the day-to-day. Truly, I had no hope of *not* being all in. I am not a person who can simply participate in something or who can stand by watching something cry for attention and not get it. To the contrary, I'm very much a "fixer" and problem solver.

So, a month after I'd put on skates, when someone stepped down from our board of directors—the group charged with guiding the di-rection of our league—I said I would serve out that term.

That was in mid-March. And before it felt like I had a chance to even think about it, I was on our board for the next five years. I served as a trainer and a captain. I cosigned a loan, had my name registered on the LLC. Then, at a certain point, I eased out of leadership for Ohio Roller Derby a bit in order to take on more responsibility with the WFTDA. That ended up with me serving as the membership officer for four years, then being elected to a two-year term as vice president. You know, classic stuff that someone who doesn't want to be in charge would do.

I failed royally on the second resolution. And while it was so hard at times, I don't regret that part at all.

We split our league into four home teams during those early days. Most teams did this at the time; the prospect of playing against teams in other cities was still a while off from being a possibility, much less the norm, so the word *league* is confusingly used in the sport of roller derby. You have a "local league" in a city that might be made up of sev-eral home teams or might operate on more of a varsity/junior varsity, A/B-team model. Those leagues are often members of our governing body, the WFTDA, originally named the United Leagues Coalition, which sounds like some sort of superhero consortium. And it kind of was, in terms of creating roller derby infrastructure.

Our four home teams lived up to the early modern derby aesthetic as well.

The Band of Brawlers was a military-themed team with a Band of Brothers pun name. Their pleated camo skirts flew up to show a hot pink lining when they fell; The Blackeye Bullies wore black and blue, and usually sported fake black eyes; The Sprockettes sported a baby blue (later purple) and silver '50s-inspired, outer-space-themed look. They constructed a giant cardboard UFO to emerge from at our first game.

And finally, my team, The Take-Outs: red-and-gold ninjas with a takeout Chinese-food-box-on-wheels logo. I'd be remiss if I didn't acknowledge how very problematic and culturally appropriative our team's theme was. Originally, we were supposed to be kind of Chinese food delivery-driver themed, but then it morphed into all things Asian/ninja/kung fu, and so on, as if an entire continent none of us had ties to was homogenous. We posed with swords and chopsticks and had a ninja-costumed mascot. I absolutely cringe at it all now, and it's hard to believe that such a short time ago it somehow read "kitsch" to us rather than "cringey" at best, or more like downright racist at its worst. Could it have been rebranded with the same name and remade into something inoffensive? Probably. Do I wish we would have?

Absolutely.

As a league, we were nothing if not ambitious. OHRD's first season was held in Battelle Hall, part of the Greater Columbus Convention Center. It was a huge, open room with a concrete floor, and the last time I had been in it prior to our first game was my freshman year of college for a Nine Inch Nails concert. This was no roller rink afternoon game. To the contrary, we had a professional sound system, and at one point in the season, professional lighting that we were still paying for a full year later. That first game was one of the largest crowds I've skated in front of, even to this day, and the crowd was a motley mix of friends and family, aspiring skaters from leagues starting up throughout Ohio, aging punk rockers, elderly folks who remembered derby's heyday, and even a couple of folks from Chicago's Windy City Rollers who drove in and guested on the announcers' mic that night. I still meet people who were there that night and never came to another game.

I only remember a few things from that night:

- My very first action was to skate out during our introductions and trip on the rope lights, falling directly to the ground.

- At one point, I desperately and purposely fell in front of opposing jammer Dirty Mother Trucker and feared expulsion, wondering what on earth had come over me.

- My uncle, who plugged his ears with toilet paper from the bathroom due to the loud volume, informed me at the end of the game that I had fallen 11 times. I only remembered the aforementioned 2.
- The atmosphere felt like a circus.
- My team won.

There were five more double-header games that season, culminating in the Envy Cup Championship. People retired midseason, new skaters were drafted, we made money, paid bills, broke even, lost money, practiced, attended open skates at Skate Zone, scrimmaged at United Skates, guzzled beer after practice, fought among ourselves, made best friends, had a great time—all the things you expect in any young business, any large group of people who are getting to know each other while also working toward a common goal.

That November we were invited by the Minnesota Rollergirls in St. Paul to play them at the Legendary Roy Wilkins Auditorium, which is still one of the best venues in our sport. We eagerly accepted the invitation and started to work on creating an all-star team, the best of the best of our four home teams, who would face off against the MNRG All-Stars. While Minnesota had years of experience compared to us, our coaches convinced us this was a very winnable game.

This resulted in us being supremely overconfident. When I look back at the score now (142–55 for Minnesota), it wasn't nearly as bad as we interpreted it to be at the time, especially considering the difference between our expectations of officiating and what we got when we played the game—and also the fact that we had absolutely no experience. We were used to serving penalties and having our opponents do so as well. We entered the game nervous about having a penalty-prone player foul out. But to the contrary, in this game, a grand total of *one* player served *one* penalty minute, when one of our opponents grabbed me around the waist and barrel-rolled both of us into the Ohio spectators sitting trackside. No one else went to the box for the entire game.

Considering we regularly had folks getting to foul-out numbers in our home games, to say that this was surprising to us was an understatement. We were not used to having to adjust on the fly, and we did not do so. I can see all of that now. But at the time, we didn't have the hindsight necessary, and the result of that game, as well as our feelings about it, would hang over our heads for seasons to come.

In those early days, teams would negotiate before games using something called the "Discrepancy-O-Matic," which was ostensibly to help standardize the house rules that each league used in order to make it an even playing field. It was a worksheet with questions—for example: Is passing the jammer a point? Can you legally pass an opponent out of bounds? Is there a penalty wheel to spin for an extra punishment when someone goes to the box? Such basics had to be hashed out before a game was played. There was a standard rules set that WFTDA published, and theoretically that's what we all played under, but there were differences in interpretation running rampant from team to team. Newer skaters are sometimes boggled when I explain this kind of negotiation because the rules simply *are* to them. And it's not until they see the revision process in person, and see that all leagues contribute to all changes as new versions are published, that they realize we were *all* making this entire sport up, together, while we competed among ourselves and with each other.

3 False Start

If I had been told as a kid that someday I would break my back while consensually participating in a full-contact sport, I would have guffawed. I don't use that word lightly. *Guffaw* feels like a clunky exaggeration in most contexts, but I know with complete certainty that had someone walked up to fifth-grade me—a freckled bookworm with a snotty vocabulary and nonstop craving for Cheetos Puffs—if someone had whispered, "Sam, put down that book about the Bermuda Triangle, do I have a story for you," I would have guffawed. I would have brayed like a little blonde, clumsy, sports-avoidant donkey.

I never had any sports heroes. My little brother, Ronnie, had them all. Ronnie collected special edition Wheaties boxes, football books and mugs and pencils and towels, Colorado Rockies playing cards, posters of the best basketball players in the world. He pretended to win the Heisman, practiced end zone dances, and openly sobbed when the Broncos won back-to-back Super Bowls in '98 and '99. This always occurred on a Dad's-house weekend, and Dad required us to take to the streets clanging pots and pans and cheering as though he were toothy Elway himself.

Sunday football was Ronnie's and Dad's religious experience. My sister, Daisy, and I waited out Super Bowls in the kitchen, lounged by the wings and cheese and Vienna sausage platter, dreaming of *X-Files* reruns or, perhaps, a long walk at the nature center. If Daisy and I wanted to emulate exceptional female athletes, we wouldn't get much further than the sensationalized nightly news portrayals of Nancy or Tonya. We weren't shown women with athletic prowess; we were offered soapy drama instead.

I internalized a specific cultural message about athletics: not for girls. It wasn't that I hated sports; it was more like sports had little to do with me, a girl. As fast and fearless as I was at the skating rink, carving in and out of lesser skaters and their widdle baby safety walkers, I couldn't find my place in team sports. It wasn't for lack of trying. I played coed YMCA basketball throughout elementary school, ran line sprints, and double-dribbled across the newly carpeted gymnasium. Though I was a hustler—a sweaty, red-faced 10-year-old unafraid of occasional rugburn, faster than my babyface implied—I spent most of my time benched with the other 3 girls on our team of 15.

My lack of playing time did not deter the enthusiasm of my young, incidentally feminist, single mother.[1] She reinforced my competitive nature with bleacher howls and unwavering encouragement, the loudest parent in the gym. This was not sports-specific. She offered the same public displays of validation at spelling bees (*That's okay, Sam! "Forest" sure sounds like a double-R word!*), school plays (*That's my Sammy! The star of the show!*), and knowledge bowls (*Nobody can English like MY baby!*). Mom came to every single one of my games, which eventually made way for theater productions—as a kid, I could not find any sport to play as well as I could project to the back of an auditorium. I'm loud, like my mother: the beautiful, curly-haired Korean American woman screaming at the coach and needing to know why her baby wasn't getting put on the court.

"Why aren't you putting Samantha in? She is fast and you better start playing her if you want to win. Why are the boys playing more?" Mom demanded. I could hear her interrogations from the locker room, where I hid until she finished avenging me. Later, in the safety of our silver 1980s Toyota van, I expressed mild displeasure at Mom's public display, and she laughed.

"You'll be fine, Sam," Mom promised. "Walk it off."

---

1   I remember the two other female athletes we idolized in the '90s: Jackie Joyner-Kersee and Flo Jo! I remember Mom screaming, "GO, Sammy—Go like Flo Jo!"

"Walk it off" may be the single lesson I retained from my short experience of being a girl in sports—and the phrase, at its core, is kinda, well, it's anti-girl. Anti-feminine, or what is culturally *perceived* as feminine. I'd heard coaches say it to boys when the insinuations were "the pain will ease soon, so stop thinking about it already and don't make a whole thing of it."

Another translation:

"Hey! Boys don't cry and I'm emotionally incompetent because of the patriarchy."

When my mom said "walk it off," I think she actually meant "Get up and keep getting up. It's going to be more difficult for you anyway, Girl Athlete, so get used to it." I wish adults would stop speaking in broken metaphors so that future adults might make better choices, because I think what I heard instead was "Don't be a wuss." Wuss-dom—the state of being a wuss—only applied to my damaged understanding of the tenets of girlhood. Being a wuss was equated with being feminine. Or being a girl. And girls didn't play sports, as far as I could see, because sports were marketed to boys, who were told to stop being wusses, which is likened to being like a girl.[2]

All of this gender stuff was confusing and inflexible and reinforced my idea that sports had little to do with *me*.

Does this mean I sucked my first go-round at the world's best sport because culture taught me girls in sports are not to be taken seriously?[3] Perhaps. Maybe I botched my first attempt at roller derby because the game is often played in what some may consider costume, by women or nonbinary folks who defy, complicate, and subvert gender, and this wasn't something 2010 me was able to critically assess. Rather than contemplate these gender subversions, I saw swagger and confidence and something to covet. I wanted in, immediately. I did not choose the rolling, full-contact sport intending athleticism; I was looking for a new identity. I tried on derby,

---

2   A word from Amy Spears: I, too, remember this phrase. In fourth grade, I stepped in a hole while playing soccer in gym class and was told to walk it off. So I did. Hours later, I was pushed out of the school to my dad's pickup truck on the secretary's office chair with a very swollen ankle. Later it was determined said ankle was fractured in two places.

3   Serena Williams for President.

like a costume, to distract myself from the pain, the rage, the war of losing my brother.

I have tethered the worst period in my life to the best sport in the world because it is how I remember the time: destruction, then derby. In 2008, the stock market crashed, so that was a thrill. My then fiancée and I had left New York City for Colorado hoping familial proximity might insulate us from complete financial despair. Freddie Mac and Fannie Mae weren't your aunt and uncle in Podunk, Nebraska, but the largest mortgage companies in the country—the companies that illegally high-blocked the economy, dragging the rest of us to the penalty box with them. Some brothers named Lehman put the world market in a chokehold—an offense worthy of game ejection—then investment banking stopped being a thing before we could understand what it was in the first place. I was 23 and trying to plan a bargain bin wedding while applying to every single job available. I couldn't land any of them. I had graduated from college in 2006, with that theater degree, yes, I know. But in 2008, everyone was firing, no one was hiring, and ill-timed rhymes made everything that much worse. In 2008, the same year Flo Rida released the single "Low," health insurance in America was as elusive, exotic, as it had ever been, and many of us hung all our frantic hopes and dreams on the potential of our first Black president.

Then, in the spring of 2008, just two weeks after I had abandoned my New York City dreams and returned to Colorado to mourn and reassess my life goals, my brother was killed in Iraq.

I thought of nothing else, the phrase on loop in my brain as if I could make sense by thinking it once more: My brother was killed in Iraq.

My family was gutted. We had unquestioningly served in the military for more than three generations, not due to patriotism so much as inheritance. And both my grandmothers were war brides, having met my grandads while the men were on duty in Korea and Germany. Suddenly, everything I thought I knew stopped making sense. What does *on duty* mean if it's in the service of state-sanctioned violence? How much say did my grandmothers have in their own lives, when war both made them poor and also provided their only op-portunity for upward mobility? How would my family continue to exist after my brother was killed in Iraq? Would my family even exist without the unquenchable American thirst for war? Where I grew up, surrounded by three military bases and a whole lotta red, white, and blue, the army was the local, dependable employment option, a way to find stability and health insurance, to pay for college, to get out of our small town. It's near impossible to be critical of war when war is a quotidian way of life, when war is framed as not much more than work; after his death, all I could think was: Why was he there to begin with?

Why are any of us, ever?

Americans, knowing or not, bask in the luxury of war *over there*, on someone else's land. My brother was killed in Iraq—so were hundreds of thousands of Iraqi civilians just trying to live their lives. War is as constant and far-reaching as it is abstract and local. Forever and invisible. Illegally made and economically sound and mostly happening for someone else—until it isn't. I was consumed by the loss of my brother, by the loss of anyone made collateral damage by the powers that be. I stopped living in the world in an apolitical fog. I started asking questions that my family, my community, and most of the country did not want asked and could not answer.

By the time 2009 arrived, I felt like I'd never find ground again. I got married five months after the pomp and circumstance of Ronnie's military funeral. He had turned 21 a month before his death, his generous laugh and deep, steady love now gone, forever. The direction of my life dissipated. All in time for the Great Recession—the greatest, one of the best, truly. I floated from job interview to job interview to job interview, competed for part-time administrative work with laid-off, middle-aged engineers. Student loans came in hot and rent started coming in hotter. Jesse, my dependable, kind, brand-new husband, had no clue how to approach my endless grief. He gave me long, silent hugs, and fed me when I wanted to eat. He, too, struggled to get work.

We bought everything secondhand and broke our lease on a cute downtown cottage to move into subsidized housing. Most evenings, I crumbled on our thrift store couch and cried. I relented to a part-time job with the Boy Scouts and failed at hiding my liberalisms (despite the extensive aforementioned training in acting). I drove my car and cried. I stopped looking into Zumba classes, I stopped hiking and dancing altogether, I got tattoos I couldn't afford because my brother was killed in Iraq. My grief left me untethered, left me in desperate need of something solid, tangible. I needed lightness and purpose, ease and power.

Skate City's rink on Academy Boulevard in Colorado Springs smells vaguely of cardboard pizza and feet. Though these might be the same smell, overlapping, it is surely the familiar smell of all skating rinks in America. The inner rink walls are tall and blue shag, early proponents of safety carpet in unexpected places. Everything else gleams cinderblock white or painted neon, an occasional ballet barre bolted waist high for people in need of additional support. On skates, I am not one of those people.

I can't recall why I decided to attend an adult speed skate night at Skate City. I don't remember much of 2009–10 because I spent most of it in a tearful blur. Adulting was hell, and the past looked better than ever. It was a relief to find Skate City as I'd left it, though Ace of Base was replaced by that Flo Rida split-in-half song, demanding, still, that I get low contextually appropriate, as I was much farther from the floor, playing limbo at 20-something rather than 5.

Every late Thursday evening, an eclectic group of roller skaters paid around six bucks to skate fast and learn to skate faster. The group, casually led by a former near-Olympic speed skater, featured women anywhere from 18 to 50-something, and few dudes other than our volunteer instructor. Some folks had previously speed skated on ice, others wore in-lines against my better judgment, but the majority rocked quads. I am humiliated to admit I sported white high-top disco wheels to the first speed skate practice I attended. I bought them at the thrift store for five bucks. It was a real amateur, dumbass move. The instructor looked at my skates, then my face, and my skates again. His eyes bugged a bit; I believe he was forcing himself not to roll them clear to the back of his head. He mumbled something about ankles. I got the point. Red-faced, and flop-sweating, I disco'd over to the skate rental counter for a more practical, appropriate boot.

What followed was an exercise in controlled chaos. Effective skating form is about precision, but where precision was lacking, I excelled in reckless optimism. I couldn't be bothered with form when all I desired was to move fast, and faster. If proper skating evoked the tenets of science, then I chose to be a science decliner. To be clear, I am not a science denier—I can acknowledge the usefulness of understanding distribution of weight, core strength in relation to body control, muscle names and muscle memory, general rules of physics, the kind of details doctors and engineers and mathematicians and (I later realized) serious athletes consider, all in the efforts of working smarter, not harder.[4] At the time, however, I was full up on grief and determined to outpace it.

"Bend your knees," our leader called across the rink. Over the speakers, Flo Rida insisted "Shorty got low, low, low, low, low, low, low, low." Imagine the difference between a steel rod and, well, a steel rod with several well-placed hinges. Imagine the unbending rod pushing, vertically upright but horizontally shoving through all that atmosphere. The hinging rod, instead, bends and glides through space, rides the horizon, uses its surroundings instead of fighting against it. I heard the instructor remind us, again, knees should remain soft, bent, the body nearer to the floor. I heard him say, "Keep your back at 45 degrees, drive your legs out laterally rather than forward and back." I heard all of this. I retained nothing. My head and heart and hinges stayed, hijacked by a single, relentless thought.

My brother was killed in Iraq.

As we queued to skate the diamond—the fastest way around an oval, cutting in tight to the short curves, gaining speed at the lengthy edges of track—several tattooed women noticed my inelegant speed, like a headless chicken on wheels, my natural talent in occasional stopping without the use of a wall or my face. As we stood in line, we

---

4   My stepdad, a third-degree blackbelt in karate, had tried to explain the physics of body work to me before. One time he expertly kicked a wooden spoon my stepbrother, Brandon, held in his hand. Stepdad broke it in half and scared the hell out of Bran and this anecdote is unrelated but it's what I recall instead of any physics lesson.

stretched to remain warm and limber for the next race whistle. I was working out a leg cramp when one of the coolest women I'd ever seen mentioned the Pikes Peak Derby Dames.

What I knew about roller derby was very little. I had spent the previous Halloween as a roller derby player. *Whip It* had recently premiered in theaters, featured Elliot Page after his success in *Juno*, and I was feeling the vibe. My costume, all thrifted, was fashioned with a distressed red/orange shirt, spandex shorts, glitter tights, and psychedelic socks. In the musty racks, I discovered that first speed skate practice pair of ridiculous shin-high '70s disco skates, as white as the cocaine folks snorted prior to disco skating. I purchased a sheet of fake tattoos and wet-ragged them onto my forearms, and to bring it home, Sharpie-scrawled a derby name across the back of my sweater-turned-jersey. I would be known as CRIMSON WAVE. I knew the clever period joke alone would make that Halloween a success.[5]

I had no real understanding of women's flat track roller derby as a full-contact sport. It was easy to get caught up in the attire, in the eyeliner and ripped stockings, in the punny skater names, in the overall theatrical aesthetic of the sport. But above all else, modern-day roller derby is a rule-heavy, legitimate and not performed, full-contact sport. The sport can be as physically and mentally demanding as, say, outpacing a global financial crisis or coping with the hideous fallout of war, but unlike money or justice, flat track roller derby is real. Like, *real* real. When I first learned of the Pikes Peak Derby Dames, it was approximately five years after the modern-day Women's Flat Track Derby Association formed, the now international governing body of our sport. It was also several decades after the performative, pro-wrestling-inspired, banked-track version that could be witnessed after Saturday morning cartoons. My Halloween costume was directly and inaccurately influenced by those Saturday morning observations. And so, when the very cool woman approached, I thought fondly on my Halloween rhetorical choices. Sam as Crimson Wave communicated "I'm sexy, I'm sassy, but I will not hesitate to beat your ass."

The words *sexy* and *sassy* rounded out my facile understanding of roller derby players, so when the very cool woman added "Tryouts are

---

5   Who doesn't love a good period joke. Or several.

here, at Skate City, in a month," I dared to picture myself as a derby player in a variety of situations. Me, with my helmet covered in anti-war slogans and maybe, also, a unicorn sticker. Me, at a bar, clothed in punk rock, having survived great loss—but in a sexy, ass-beating sort of way.

"I'll be there," I said.

And because I was 25 and lost and mourning my brother, I went home and purchased $650 of gear with a credit card, equal to the amount of a month's rent in my subsidized apartment. I ordered Riedell quad skates and knee and elbow pads and wrist guards and a mouth guard. I ordered a sticker of a Gold Star Flag, a military service flag showing I'd lost someone at war, a real conversation starter of a sticker, and I slapped it on top of a sleek, black helmet. Later, I paid too much for the very same flag, quarter-sized, tattooed on the delicate inside of my wrist. I was ready for combat, which is an inappropriate and ludicrous phrasing given my brother, Iraq, antiwar radicalization, et cetera, but it's how I felt when I suited up and practiced skating in our dinky apartment's galley kitchen. I was ready for a potential new identity, even if I had to buy it in installments.

My husband, Jesse, was confused but supportive, ready for anything that might ease my grief, or at least redirect it. He did not scold my impulse buy. He suggested inspired derby names, like "Toxic Shock" or "Beast Infection." He seemed relieved at my new sense of purpose.

My mother was extremely annoyed.

"You don't have health insurance, Sam," she said, and sighed as though she might blow the idea away altogether. My family was not doing well, all of us floundering to find a new normal in a world post-Ronnie. The toll his death took on Mom was beyond measure, and so we all did what we could to soften other possible blows. The last thing I wanted was to create more worries for Mom. That said, I was determined to manage my own despair, even if it entailed new dangerous hobbies as a coping mechanism.

I promised Mom I'd be careful, reminded her I'd had no health insurance since I turned 18. Missing health insurance was no great deterrent. Being uninsured in America is as American as being uncritical of the imperialist disaster that is America.

OHIO PLAYER PROFILE: THE WIZARD

In 2019, I watched Elektra Magneto defend her PhD in mathematics education. Most of the people in the room would never know her by Elektra, but calling her Carolyn seems wrong to me. I did not understand a large portion of Elektra's lecture, the explanation of her research on mathematics tutelage (a word, truly), but I came prepared for the Q&A, mostly hoping she'd call on me in front of the group of distinguished professors and say, "Your question, Kegel?"

If you're going to bet, bet on Elektra—who, without missing a beat, blinked hard and called

Carolyn "Elektra" Johns
(Credit: Candace Moser Stafford)

me "Sam." She remembered not to call me Vaginal Strengthening Exercise because she is the most efficient, competent person I know. I believe I witnessed a faint smirk on her face when she said my legal name, her nod to my ineptitude, the inability of anyone to catch her unguarded.

Elektra has now endured several hip surgeries, keeping her out of play for the moment, but is so dedicated to the league, the sport, that she has taken on the head coaching role of our competitive team. Elektra is loyal and reliable. Elektra is calm. Sometimes she is so calm, so cerebral, she seems a bit unavailable, but notices all. In her constant efforts at self-perfection, her latest short-term goal is "to have fun." She finds quizzing players on game rules fun. She enjoys producing short videos teaching derby strategy and posting them on our forums. She uses cat toys and narrates pretend game play as her main dude, Martin the tuxedo cat, watches from a box in the background. "Martin is in the penalty box," she says. When the team offers Elektra feedback, we congratulate her on having fun.

Pull back the curtain. The person there, surrounded by laptops and cats lounging on binders of Excel spreadsheets and meeting minutes, is sly Elektra. Elektra looks like she was engineered in a Swiss lab, White but poolside tan, blonde, blue eyed, her hair in a ropey milkmaid pony or piled on her head because she has no time for that shit. Some dummies might underestimate someone so pretty. It is safer to assume Elektra will be awake before and after the rest of us, preparing for world domination as she also battles a migraine or a sports-related hernia.

Have I mentioned Elektra's love of Disney and musicals?

If there is a committee (there are, forever endless Ohio Roller Derby committees), Elektra is on it, has been on it, wrote a proposal for it, changed the bylaws or policy of it, or knows exactly where to find the correct documentation for it. Ask, and ye shall receive a direct, flat, and thorough response. And, if you are deserving, a faint smirk for (1) caring to ask and (2) knowing who will find the answer. To earn that smirk is to feel on top of the world.

Don't mistake her for a humorless taskmaster, even when she is one. She is a policy wonk, takes pleasure in order and consistency; these qualities make her invaluable as a coach and trainer. There is no greater joy than when Elektra is on the track, jamming and juking around my incessant ass, and I somehow manage to catch her—using the precise directions she gave me on how to catch her.

Bend low, move laterally, stop turning sideways.

Once, I caught her with the edge of my right hip, managed to push her just outside of bounds, and I was rewarded with the most maniacal laughter. Elektra's laugh is startling, sort of evil in its joy. It is hard earned, and I knew in that moment that Elektra's joy was not in my tardy application of skill, but because she had orchestrated it altogether.

—Kegel Scout

A Word from Amy Spears, Roller Derby Historian

"Get small to get big" is a slogan that we coined about halfway through the process it describes. Basically, as an organization, Ohio Roller Girls was buying into several myths and had been for some time. One was that we were bigger than we actually were. Not in stature, but in quantity of skaters. To the contrary, we know how small we are physically. At 5'6" on a good day, I am absolutely one of our taller players. I'm sure we could field an entire roster's worth of skaters 5'3" or shorter with no issues. But this was a more philosophical kind of getting smaller.

At the time of our very first game, yes, we had 60 skaters, four teams of 15 each. But we weren't being honest about what that really meant. There were injuries and illnesses, vacations and job travel, so it wasn't like we truly had 60 skaters who could hit the track at any given time. One team was chronically short-staffed and therefore always seemed to get the lion's share of rookies. We didn't have the person power we kept telling ourselves we did.

Compounding this was some of us had gotten bitten by the interleague bug. The prospect of traveling and competing against skaters who weren't the same folks we practiced and scrimmaged with day in and day out was so much more exciting than the same four teams competing every summer (and the same ones always winning, as The Take-Outs three-peated our annual championships). Having to play home teams for part of the year, then jump straight into all-stars season with no break, and the fact that the interleague "season" was now starting to have a shape nationally—it was all starting to wear some of us down.

Add to that the fact that a lot of us were doing double or triple duty—playing the sport, acting as trainers, being on the board, or leading committees, and oh yeah, day jobs that actually paid money rather than taking it—something had to give.

A lot of roller derby teams say that their home season is what pays for their travel season. They say local fans are used to those home teams and have allegiances, and they aren't as interested when the skaters are all mashed up into an all-stars team to play someone from out of town. I have no doubt that's true in some places, especially those early teams who had those home systems set up before roller derby existed on a national (now international) level. But we started playing other cities so early on that our fans didn't have time to build those allegiances to home teams before they started rooting for Ohio against Naptown (Indianapolis) or Cincinnati or Steel City (Pittsburgh).

That sounds weird, right? Ohio versus Cincinnati? It's a testament to how short-sighted so many of us were about how fast our sport would grow that we claimed the names of entire states to describe our teams early on. Texas Rollergirls are from Austin; Minnesota Roller Derby, St. Paul. We were following the trend as the first in our state when we put the entirety of Ohio in our moniker rather than being the Columbus Rollers or some such thing. But also, Columbus has no well-known, definitive nickname. So it's still Ohio. Our charter team—the one that plays for rankings—still has no name independent of our league. On one hand, that's great because who else do we represent but our league-mates. On the other, it would be nice to have an identity to get behind, like a Naptown Tornado Siren or a member of the 5280 Fight Club from Denver. Alas, we have a name that in another sport would sound as generic as "City Basketball."[6] But in roller derby, it's kind of normal.

In any case, the way we were weird is that our fans knew Ohio Roller Derby as their team, more so than any of our home teams. So at the end of that third season, one of our coaches and I started re-searching and putting together a proposal. Other leagues had already done what we were thinking: dissolving their home teams and feeding everyone into an A/B system. We were definitely not the first, so in the true DIY spirit of roller derby, we asked for help from those who had been there. And later, we offered it as well, sharing our proposals and plans with other leagues who asked.

It's hard for me to convey how deeply this affected some people. A decent-sized cohort of our skaters were dead set against this plan, as they didn't see where they'd fit. They either didn't think they were good enough and would never be able to play, or they thought we were trying to get people to quit or kick people out. I imagine several thought I was feeding them a line when I tried to convince them it would be so much easier to train and improve in this format. And it was hard to commu-nicate how deeply I felt I could not go on in our current system. And I wasn't alone. I was just more vocal about it. We never had a break. Never scheduled time off from practices other than maybe one week at Christ-mas and one around the Fourth of July. I didn't feel like I could take my own break or take a vacation, or do anything other than roller derby. Our

---

6   The trend of professional soccer teams declaring themselves "XYZ Foot-ball Club" makes me feel a little better about this.

first-ever league-wide break was scheduled in July 2009—a full four *years* after we started practices. I honestly felt that if our proposal wasn't voted in, I was probably going to have to transfer to another league and drive about an hour to Dayton—the next closest city that already had an A/B system. Quitting wasn't even a thought, because roller derby is what I did now. It was around the same time that I had made the choice to ditch the derby name I'd used for our first couple seasons—Alli Catraz—and use my real name instead. People wanted to attach all sorts of reasons to my decision regarding legitimacy of the sport, but it was honestly because I recognized then that derby was a part of my life, my real life, and I didn't feel like the wearing of a persona was for me anymore. So there was no way I could leave. But something had to give.

Compounding my stress regarding the team structure decision was the fact that this proposal was being presented and voted on right around the time of our board elections, and our founder had already announced she wasn't running for another term as league president. I had already decided I was going to run for that position, partially because I felt I had to, but mostly because I did believe I could steer this ship and that someone had to step up to do so. And because, as I have mentioned, this is what I do. I end up in charge.

My platform was firmly built on the prospect of whittling down to two teams, while my opponent presented an alternate plan that took us from four home teams to three and kept the two interleague teams as well without explaining how that would help, other than it would disband The Take-Outs, who'd won all three championships, were mostly made up of the longest-term players, and were most of the ones vocally in favor of my proposal.

There's a lot of emotional turmoil I've forgotten from this time, or that maybe I've pushed down deep somewhere unreachable. Ultimately, my version of the proposal passed and our home teams were disbanded. I was elected league president as well. I was incredibly nervous about this and had gone out with my best friend to distract myself on the evening the results were to be announced. When I read the email on my phone, I was so relieved the election was over I ordered an expensive bourbon and ended up accidentally royally hungover the next day, as I faced the uphill battle of what I now had to do.

As a result of the team restructure, a small group of people did leave. The myth persists to this day that all of them left because of the disbanding of those teams, but I think many of them would admit now that they were done whether or not that had panned out. A few had nagging injuries, or wanted to start families, or had kids getting older and more involved in their own extracurriculars. Some of those folks that left didn't talk to me for a long time, but most of them attended later games as fans and came around emotionally, and I count them among friends now. A couple returned to skate in later years and recognized it was the right decision for our organization—because it meant we were there to come back to later, when we might not have been otherwise. One or two of those who stuck around didn't get exactly what they expected, but contrary to the worries before the decision was made, it wasn't the lower-level players who had expected not to play but rather the ones who were already on the travel team, and maybe burned themselves out further, or weren't ready for the competition as leaguemates improved.

I don't remember ever hearing a real-life person seriously use the word *burnout* before roller derby. And even then, for years, we acted like this wasn't a thing. To say it wasn't healthy would be a severe understatement. We didn't at all consider that attrition was a thing that should be expected or that it was normal. Shortsightedness, youth, the hubris of a few overly passionate, single-minded folks—whatever the reason, it was assumed that leaving roller derby wasn't at all to be considered. In fact, the very first retirement form our league's leadership distributed had a signature line acknowledging that after retirement, you'd still be required to volunteer. It didn't ask *if* you wanted to; it asked *which* job you wanted to perform. I'm reasonably certain it was intended to mean you had to volunteer to remain a voting member, but it sounded more like you had committed for life. It made it seem that leaving the track meant signing your own indenture, pledging to tape track or sweep floors for the rest of your days.

We even had an early coach who seemed to regard the need to step away as a sort of moral failing. I don't blame or judge him for this now—I don't honestly think he thought this, no matter how hard he projected it. But there was certainly an unspoken assumption that there was no other valid desire than to continue playing roller derby, barring that as a possibility to continue playing roller derby. Having a baby? Here's how you come back. Broken leg? Here's what you do after physically healing. Moving away? How dare you! But also, here's the contact info for the team in your new city; let me write you a letter of recommendation.

We loved it so much, so passionately, that we couldn't dream of not having it. So allowing an exit strategy felt like denigrating what we were building.

Though we couldn't admit it or talk about it, the truth was there is an end to the career of most roller derby skaters. And at the end of season three, we were hitting the natural point where some skaters wanted to do something else. So while some folks from that era of Ohio Roller Girls refer to us disbanding the home team as "The Split"—a shorthand for the thing that happened to so many leagues early on when they split into two leagues because of irreconcilable differences—it actually was probably something more like "The Merger," when we finally became one organization. It was a point in the natural ebb and flow of things that meant it was time for change. But a wound would remain either way, the emotional scars of *feelings* making their way into roller derby.

The rest of "get small to get big" happened in those next few seasons. All those times we'd told ourselves we had 60 skaters but didn't really? That wasn't just how we were budgeting players, but money as well. While we were doing okay financially, especially when contrasted with some other leagues who were our contemporaries, we still were squeaking by. We had some debt. We had played our first season at the convention center and then moved to the ever-so-slightly cheaper state fairgrounds. We hadn't anticipated some electrical costs that had come along with the professional lighting for our second game and still had that on a credit card. And at the end of our second season, we'd purchased a floor to lay down over the slick concrete, thinking that would solve all our issues of constant falling at our new venue. We would pay that off over the next five years.

After season four, during my second year-long term as president and with Phoenix Bunz as our treasurer spearheading the plan, we made a huge decision that at the time seemed terrifying. Instead of holding our games in this high production value venue and making use of that expensive floor we were paying off, Bunz proposed we move our games to a much smaller, grungier, and, importantly, significantly cheaper—like 90 percent cheaper—roller hockey rink. There was no seating, bare-bones bathrooms, not all that much parking. It was in an industrial area near an inner-suburban neighborhood. We knew it was slated to be torn down for the upcoming mixed-use development Grandview Yard in a few years, so it was guaranteed to be temporary. The heating and cooling was not much to speak of. And the scariest part—they didn't have a license to sell beer.

But, with our core fans, mostly friends and family, we could sell it out every time—provided they'd still attend without beer. Our profit margin would increase drastically. We could pay everything off then, hopefully, go back to a bigger venue in a few years in much better financial shape.

The second part of "get small to get big" was less intuitive to most people: we needed to raise the bar on tryouts and who we allowed to come in as new skaters to the league. While we hadn't had the "walk in the door and do your falling drills" policy that I came in under since that very first season, we still had open recruitment and even multiple tryouts every year. We basically still took everyone who showed up to tryouts, thinking we could mold them into derby players after they decided that was the thing they truly wanted—and that was true to a certain extent. But it also meant we usually had a small group of folks who weren't quite able to pass minimum skills. They were at practices, at least sporadically, but they never got to play games because they couldn't commit to enough practices to make a roster. They got discouraged when they weren't able to immediately fulfill their derby dreams, which served to stunt their progress and crush their motivation. It might have felt better to say yes on tryouts nights than "Hey, not yet," but we didn't have the training personnel—nor time—to be able to get them up to speed. We weren't setting them up for success in the long run. It didn't feel fair to keep taking their dues if they weren't going to get the glory.

We revamped tryouts. We added off-skates fitness testing. By this point, we'd set up a recreational league, so we were able to point those folks who didn't make it toward roller derby and not cut them off completely, letting in only the folks who could truly hit the ground skating and who were likely to be roster ready within their first year. And as a result, we ended up with fewer skaters overall. That might seem like it was the wrong choice or like it was counterintuitive, with the reduced dues income as a result, but it panned out. We had a more stable number of skaters, so our finances were more predictable than they ever had been.

By 2012, we were able to pay off all of our debts. And at the end of that time, having hit the reset button and being able to make better budgeting decisions, we ended up going back to our larger venue again, this time with the ability to make a small profit after operating costs.

Whether we knew it overtly, we were setting the stage for getting big in another way, as we spent the next few seasons rising in the WFTDA ranks and becoming a team who could truly compete in roller derby's rapidly expanding international playing field.

4 Fresh Meat

Pike's Peak Roller Derby tryouts happened in March 2010, right around the time Ronnie would have turned 23—the age I was when he left for the desert, and never came back. I took this as some sort of convoluted sign and decided I must make the team in memory of Ronnie, the biggest sports fan I'd ever known. I imagined him laughing his ass off at his big sister, rolling around, getting hit for the hell of it. My husband, Jesse, and I brainstormed derby names for months, and we considered Ronnie's missing, missed, reaction to each of them. I'd quickly quit riding the Crimson Wave, because it seemed too . . . easy? Feral Streep[1] was a personal favorite, but Jesse assured me Ronnie would much prefer Beast Infection.[2]

I arrived 20 minutes early to tryouts, though I kept referring to it as an "audition" internally, I set up camp in the lobby, and I stretched as if athletics were a thing I did. Another skater sat close to the rink entrance, pulling on her own gear. She already looked the part, a spray

---

1 Later taken up by a roller derby friend and writer in Ohio.

2 As the sport has evolved and grown, some teams and players choose to use their actual names—this, in an effort to be taken more seriously by a larger audience. Most, however, have decided against changing the happy weirdo culture of roller derby. Derby people are nonconformist, which is often how they arrived at derby in the first place. Is there anything more legitimate than getting body checked by an Oxford Coma or a Hardkore or Blitz Lemon or Smash Panda?

of bright flowers tattooed across her chest, her bangs barrel-curled to Bettie Page perfection. I wiped my own damp bangs back. I'd been sweating since always.[3]

"Are you nervous?" I asked.

She smiled, shook her head. "No, I'm excited."

"Me too," I lied. "How long have you skated?" I tried to keep a friendly tone as I sized up the competition.

"Oh, well, since I was a kid," she said, after pausing to add up the years on her hands.

"Me too. I've skated for 20 years," I said. I hate to gloat,[4] but I had counted before I'd arrived. I knew to be prepared long before I began working with Boy Scouts.

At 10 minutes 'til tryouts, more than 50 women filled the lobby. The group as a whole, heavy on the eyeliner and Hot Topic, looked fierce. We remained largely silent. A few seemed to regret their intense clothing choices, shredded or otherwise, and I congratulated myself on my plain white workout tee and yoga pants; there had been many discussions on tryout attire and etiquette at speed skate practice. Veterans, coaches, the folks with clipboards would concern themselves with skill, not style.

They called us Fresh Meat. I also heard newbies, wannabes, potential rookies, but Fresh Meat rang true. The rink I'd known and loved was alien with the fluorescents left on and throbbing overhead, no giddy strobes or spotlights, no romantic dimming to ease the tension. We stumbled out onto the rink floor and lined up, slabs of beef in a grocery deli. We huddled closer as the real skaters circled. A few of the Derby Dames rolled out in full gear, and it was then I noticed the rockabilly beauty from the lobby. She was not Fresh Meat, as I had assumed, but Prime Fucking Rib. She was the Swiss Missile, and she moved accordingly. The flowers danced across her chest, animated as she soared in graceful laps. She was not showing off. She was in her natural habitat.

I considered leaving.

The basic skills test covered skate stride and posture. We were asked to demonstrate crossovers, told to bend our knees. The first and last rule of roller derby is to bend your godforsaken knees. That's it.

---

3   In 2019 I was awarded Ohio Roller Derby's Slickest Skater Award. I'd like to thank my mother for this horrific genetic condition.

4   I do not.

You can stop reading now. Skaters were judged on stopping ability, or, at least, potential. We lined up in shaky columns to weave in and out of small orange cones, the cones continually reset as skaters rolled over and dragged them several feet. They timed our speeds on a single lap, and they set up more cones so we could attempt jumping and prove we could get at least six inches off the ground. Six inches is near the approximate height of a downed skater. If a skater struggles, from the start, to get at least that far off the ground, then the game may end up full of flailing downed skaters, piles of legs and helmets and wheels scattered across painted cement.

I did well. And compared to 97 percent of the Fresh Meat, I did really fucking well. It was clear most folks had either never been on skates or hadn't seen a skate in years. By the end of the sweaty blur, only three made the cut, and I was one.

I remember limping to my car post-tryouts, dehydrated and dazed. The Swiss Missile smiled and waved as she drove past in the parking lot.

By the end of March 2010, I had settled on the perfect derby name, a jab at the Boy Scouts for keeping me clocked at 32 hours each week—the maximum amount of time served before they legally had to provide health insurance. I called my mother with the good news.

"Hey Ma. It's me, Kegel Scout."

She snorted into the phone, probably prouder than ever.

Practices were two evenings a week, two hours at a time, and this did not include the elliptical machine, weight lifting, and plyometrics I did on my own time. I was consumed by roller derby. I watched You-Tube videos of Texas bouts. Skate City stopped being a simple throwback to my childhood and evolved into my adrenaline-inducing second home. I'd drive to practice, equal parts thrilled and terrified. We did burpees on skates, sit-ups and push-ups in full gear; we drilled form and stops and single-leg skating. We fell by accident and we fell on purpose and more than earned every single bruise, scrape, or rink rash. Then the hitting began.

It was during a mid-April practice when a veteran skater, probably frustrated with her own uninspired derby name, blew me up. She very much enjoyed nailing every rookie with more force than she ought to. My whole right side absorbed the hit, and the physics or science of movement, or whatever, kept the hateful energy moving through my body until I collapsed, full force, on my bent left knee. I yelped, and she turned back for a brief second, her face in permanent scowl, as if the world around her had spoiled. On impact, I felt something snap like a rubber band. An intense, searing pain burned through my knee when I tried to stand. I stayed down.

At a previous practice, the very same skater had announced something like, "Fresh Meat should know their place. You all are lucky you can already skate. I didn't even skate at all until a few years ago." She said roller derby was her only outlet, time for herself outside of being a mother and working the same crappy jobs we all competed for, together. Weren't we on the same team? I thought of this as I began sobbing in the middle of the rink, on the floor I'd known intimately for most of my life.

Pepper Slay, an excellent player and teammate and nurse, hurried over. "Something is wrong," I said. Pepper asked questions about the angle of the fall, the sound and feel of the injury, then slung my arm around her shoulders and helped me drag myself to the lockers.

"You know, thanks to you, I've gotta explain what a Kegel is to my eight-year-old," she joked. I kept crying.

"I don't have health insurance," I told her. Pepper winced, so I added, "Sorry about your vaginal exercise explanations."

Pepper advised rest, ice, compression, elevation, and if RICE didn't suffice, head to a doc, insured or not. I left practice early. On the drive home, I clenched my left thigh and felt a looseness in my knee I'd not had before.

I Googled my pain and figured I'd torn a ligament, something like a PCL. I tried to step into the shower, then fell over the lip of the tub when I couldn't raise my bent left leg 90 degrees in the air. When Jesse got home from work, I started crying all over again. I took the next practice off, and then the next. I did not want to tell my mom. I told her. She told Grandpa, who had been thoroughly impressed with my attempt at "Roller Ball" and offered me his yellowed, 1980s knee brace. I used it.

Ice packs and heating pads and a few missed practices got me through to early May. Ibuprofen bottles littered my apartment counters. My body, covered in fingerprint bruises and intergalactic wounds, had never felt stronger or more pained. Jesse said maybe I should take more time off, so I reminded him about the cost of gear and the credit card bill and he let me be. I was beginning to understand the amount of effort and free time these women dedicated to a sport so few people took seriously, that this was not a lifestyle or an identity to try on for size, not a replacement for therapy or the grieving process. Roller derby was not to be taken lightly. It was not easy, would never, ever be easy, which is why players drop like flies, and how I rostered for the first bout of the season, held at the historic Colorado Springs City Auditorium.

By May I'd made a few friends on the team. Despite my urging them to embrace my name in its entirety, they insisted on calling me "Scout." No one seemed eager to associate the tightening of pelvic floor muscles with the highest ranked Boy Scout. Their loss, I figured, and insisted on the full name printed in the bout program.

The Colorado Springs City Auditorium is an old gymnasium/theater, with gorgeous wood floors and balcony seating. It is used for concerts and festivals and various gatherings and feels like the kind of place that has history, which is true of very few places out west. I don't remember much of my first roller derby bout other than a lot of pre- and postgame gastrointestinal chaos and an exorbitant amount of sweating. Some of my old high school teachers came to watch and sat with my mother, who told them she had no idea what was going on. The rest of the crowd included every alternative type in the city, drinking, cheering, jeering, decked out in leather and zippers and anarchist patches. In what I hoped was a new gutsy roller derby fashion, I invited my Boy Scout coworkers to watch. I had to explain what a Kegel was to several of them, many of whom were grown-up Eagle Scouts themselves. There are countless jokes to be had here, but I am showing restraint. My boss, who knew I was a reluctant and frustrated worker in such a conservative organization, was in the stands when my entrance was announced: "Number 319, Kegel Scout!" I searched for his face as I waved to the room, then tripped on my own skate in front of several hundred people.

What I remember best about that day is feeling like a total ass. I truly had no solid grasp on the rules of the game. Most of my time on the track was hit or be hit. Women flung out against one another like flying orbs in some punk rock pinball machine, lipstick stained across arms and jerseys. I went to the penalty box once, and I know this because there is a picture of me, red cheeked and wide eyed, sitting beside a skating official. Whoever I was that day was fleeting, and this picture captured the momentary self: the panic in my face, the slouch of my shoulders, black eye makeup running down and pooling around my neck.

Because I'd been performing since I was a kid, I thought the crowd would disappear so I could focus on the action, but this was not the case. I had a funny name, I wore black-and-gold fishnets, but sport is more than spectacle. There was no script, no blocking (well, okay, a lot of blocking), and improv was not about comedic timing; rather, it was shifting left to right to dodge a magnificent person named Fanny Fister. My knee throbbed through the hour-long bout. Someone named Beaver knocked me down and then someone else with another wacky name ran me over. I ate shit more than a handful of times. I went home shaken, pretending I'd had a good time.

The next morning, I woke up feeling proud for surviving my first bout, ready to spend the day relaxing on the couch. And then, I couldn't sit up in bed.

I tried again, my palms pressed down at my sides into the mattress. Nope.

I couldn't hinge at the waist. I was, suddenly, a steel rod. I shoved a bit harder into the mattress, then squealed; a bright, white pain exploded in my lower back. I lay in bed against my will, contemplating my brief and now certainly finished turn at—what had happened, exactly? I didn't really even play much roller derby, did I?

I yelled for Jesse, who was scrambling eggs in the kitchen.

"Hey! Uh. I—Jesse. I can't get up."

He laughed, shouted, "Hang on," and took his time getting to my side, no hustle, until he saw the look of terror on my face. He opened and closed his mouth, then bent toward me.

Bending. What a gift, I thought. Together, we rolled me out of bed like a carpet, and he lifted my torso as I managed my hips and legs, my body straight and unbending, a steel rod with no hinge. I stumbled to the bathroom sink and tried to shift to a 90-degree angle without screaming.

At the time, I felt too ashamed and embarrassed to admit this might be the kind of pain I couldn't muscle through. And what more could X-rays, priced in the thousands, tell me, other than my far-fetched attempt at a derby career was over? I played roller derby for exactly three months because—well, why? Because I wanted to look cool? Because I needed a distraction? Because I was grieving, impulsively, and without health insurance?

I wouldn't confirm the broken vertebrae until four years after it happened, but the moment I slid out of bed, post-bout in May 2010, I knew my injury exceeded pulled muscle. Washing my face became a whole production, a regular Bob Fosse number, because I could not bend. Driving felt excruciating for weeks. An MRI would cost thousands of dollars, and after further consult with Dr. Google, I realized I couldn't afford physical therapy even if I had insurance. Though I knew the diagnosis, once I got around to it, would be grim, I'd make believe it was just a flesh wound and walk it off.

Lara "Rage" Arnett
(Credit: Candace Moser Stafford)

When I decided to give roller derby the old graduate school try in 2016, I attended a "Wannabe Clinic" at the United Skates of America. This was my first close encounter with Ohio Roller Derby players, who, for two hours that evening, taught a large group of women how to derby. I showed up with all the gear I'd purchased the first go-round in Colorado and worried it would send the wrong message—that I knew what I was doing. As every other participant rented skates, borrowed pads and helmets and purchased mouthguards from our instructors, I geared up quickly and avoided eye contact. I had no desire to share my derby history, because I was about to suck.

We were practicing falls—baseball slides and plow stops and t-stops—when Rage rolled over and offered kind commentary on my form. I mumbled a joke about being particularly clumsy while on my period, Rage grinned, and that's when we recognized each other. Not that we'd ever met before—it was just the kind of moment when you meet someone new and you know, with complete certainty, they are your friend. Rage felt it too, I could see. It's lucky and wonderful to finally meet the people you've known all along.

There is nothing rage-filled about Rage. Rage is zen. Their soul is as old as their energy is placid, which has nothing to do with how they play roller derby. Rage is strong, powerful, unavoidable. Like me, Rage has an obvious body. We do not fit the bullying, conventional standards we grew up with. We have both struggled with our size in a world that still insists women are valuable when they are smaller and less visible. This is not true in roller derby.

The impetus for my belated, ongoing self-acceptance was this sport. Rage has said much of the same. This was a space we both always needed, a place where a body is not judged by its outward appearance, or even its functionality or physical prowess. At its best, roller derby is fighting, hard, against the judgment of bodies altogether.

Rage demonstrates radical empathy for herself, is open and honest about their journey. Rage is awake, alive, and hopeful. Rage radiates this, and in a stretch of Ohio gray, they are what I need. Everything Rage touches grows.

Their home is verdant, lush, full of plants and homegrown vegetables and homemade spices. Rage is sweet and cozy, gorgeous, her hair daring and ever-evolving, mullet to shag to rockabilly babe and back. They have made me proud to be thick, helped me love my body as it is, however it is.

Rage's enlightened words remind me the power of visibility:

> Body changes are one of the things I struggle most to cope with. I still have deep rooted shame revolving around body stuff, fatness, weight gain, muscle loss, etc. And it's really difficult for me to come out with my feelings about my own experiences. Lately, I've felt a lot of avoidance, reclusiveness, and overall feelings of disconnect. Which feels very scary and not fun but I'm getting by and trying very hard to work through it. This year alone has been one of the most difficult because I've experienced a lot of different seasons with my vessel. Some that I perceive negatively and a lot of other changes that have helped me accomplish some really great things. Skating helps me feel safe and secure and confident. Skating helps me feel seen. And I'm so fucking thankful for the visibility of bodies like mine who shred and kick ass on the track, in the streets, and at the parks. I'm so thankful to have found my people and a sport that helps me feel empowered in my body.
>
> This is for me but also for my friends.
>
> I'm here, healing isn't linear.
>
> All bodies are good bodies.
>
> Even when sometimes It's hard to remember that about yourself.

> —Kegel Scout

A Word from Amy Spears, Who Invented Roller Derby[5]

Ohio Roller Derby plays a lot of games. A *lot* of games. We have, in fact, played more sanctioned games (the ones that count for rankings) than any other team in our sport—202 interleague games from 2006 through 2019. We've played more than Texas's 193—the Texas Rollergirls, who founded the sport and who went to playoffs and champs every single year, and who started playing interleague a year before us. After that, there is a three-way tie at 175 games between Denver, Detroit, and Philly. All of whom except Denver played their first interleague game before us. And all of whom went to postseason tournaments more years than us. A postseason usually gives you 3 to 4 games at playoffs and then another few if you make it to champs. So that puts into perspective just how many regular season games we play.

We're averaging 14 games a season, having a postseason only 10 times out of our 15 seasons, and only once getting to champs. Texas's average is about 13 games, but at least 4 of those were postseason in any given year. We play so many regular season games.

The minimum number of games WFTDA requires to qualify for ranking has varied over the years, but it's usually been around 4. Few teams play only that minimum number, but sometimes circumstances of geography and finances mean you take what you can get (or who you can get to) in terms of opponents. We're lucky in Columbus; being in the heartland means a significant number of the teams in the US and Canada are within reasonable driving distance. That gives us a lot of options for booking games.

For a number of years, the people in charge of booking the season were the same people who were running the business side of our league, being frugal and getting us out of debt. That same philosophy extended to season planning. We all foot the bill for our own travel, and we couldn't conceive of not trying to make it worth every penny our teammates were

---

5   I did not invent roller derby. Because I am acquainted with some of the people who actually did invent roller derby, I feel like I have to acknowledge that this is a blatant lie. But my teammates like to call me things like #derbygrandma and in some cases cheerfully point out I'm old enough to have actually birthed them, and telling people I invented our sport is one of the many things they say to people to explain that I just won't leave. (Affectionately, I hope.)

spending. So we made a concerted attempt to make our travel weekends have the most bang for our buck, playing hangover games in skating rinks the morning after public games, taking our charter bus on a slight detour to play a game in Madison, Wisconsin, on the way to a tournament in Milwaukee, where we played three more, and on one weekend, playing three games against three different opponents inside a 24-hour period.[6]

"Any team, anytime, anywhere" was our motto for a number of years. It saw us taking our first trip to Canada for a tournament, and it saw us playing teams ranked far above and far below us. On one occasion, when Naptown Roller Derby (Indianapolis) realized they were lacking a game to qualify for the postseason just a week before the June 30 deadline, we played them on a Wednesday night in our warehouse, most of us coming straight from work and changing from business casual to our uniforms in the grimy bathroom.

I've played most of those games. I didn't miss a game until 2010, when I separated my shoulder and realized after trying to play one game that that was a bad idea, and so I missed the next three. Then, in 2016, I took a hiatus. It was supposed to be a real break, but I ended up bench coaching. I missed getting rostered for a couple games that following year when I came back, but other than that, this has been my life for 16 years.

Overall, our team has so much game experience. Even though there's been turnover, with skaters retiring and new ones coming in, our team still has that collective experience built into our DNA. The bedrock of our culture remains in the memory of those early years, when we played so many games and yet won so few. We've let that weigh on us perhaps more, and definitely longer, than we should have.

In November 2006 we played our first interleague game in St. Paul against the Minnesota Rollergirls. We lost.

Our next interleague game was in Detroit in January 2007. We lost that one too.

Then we traveled to suburban Philadelphia for the very first East Coast Derby Extravaganza tournament in March. After our flights were

---

6   It should be noted that our charter team played three sanctioned games (Boston, Montreal, and New Hampshire) that weekend, and our B-team, Gang Green, played an additional two on this trip (Boston and Montreal). So for those crossover players we call "swingers," who play on both teams, some of them played five games within 22 hours on that trip. You play for Ohio, and you're going to get to fucking play.

canceled due to a major ice storm on the East Coast, we drove across Pennsylvania through said storm, only to lose to Windy City Rollers (Chicago) and Grand Raggidy Rollergirls (Grand Rapids, Michigan).

That same year, never being the kind of organization to back away from a challenge, we applied to host the very first eastern tournament for WFTDA. We spent most of our at-home season doing double duty by planning the tournament, dubbed Heartland Havoc. Then in August 2007, after setting up the track, securing sponsors, coordinating teams, and promoting the three-day event, just one month after the championship of our intraleague season, we faced the Rhode Island Riveters of Providence in the first round. Guess what? We lost that one too.

You are probably seeing how this is going to go for a while, so I won't bore you with the sordid details. We continued by playing a smattering of games that autumn and wouldn't see a win until we hosted our first interleague game at home in December 2007. It was a snowy day, and I remember we were a little worried that our opponents might get stranded by weather on their way from Pittsburgh. But the Steel City Derby Demons made it, and that night, for the first time ever, Ohio won an interleague roller derby game.

By three points.

The next time we won would be half a year later, in June 2008, when we beat Cleveland's Burning River at the ECDX[7] tournament.

By one point.

The hardest thing about this time was that we had players who were utterly crushed by these game results, who thought we needed to throw out everything we were doing in our training and start from scratch. And then there were folks like me who were just so happy to be playing roller derby that the outcomes didn't matter so much. The sum total of my previous sports experience was as a child and had generally included being lectured over and over that it wasn't about winning. I was in the group who felt like we just needed to keep plugging away and working hard and the success would come—eventually.

In hindsight, neither of those groups had the right answer. It wasn't really until after we disbanded those home teams and went into

---

7   After the ice storm debacle of the first year, Philly Roller Derby vowed the event would forever be hosted in warmer weather, which had the added bonus of teams getting to use the onsite pool immediately postgame from there on out.

interleague play only that our fortunes would change. During our first season without home teams, 2009, our record was eight wins and four losses. Yet, despite winning twice as many games as we lost, I don't recall the team ever feeling like we were winning or taking time to celebrate that change in fortune. I distinctly remember the stress of those games, feeling like we didn't gel, like we weren't doing well, like we were just downright bad at roller derby—smack in the middle of our first-ever multiple-game winning streak. Perfectionists all around, we had to talk about what we were doing wrong, what could be better, and we rarely mentioned the things that had gone right. In 2010, we returned to a losing season (3–7), and it felt pretty normal to us. We worked hard, but it seemed hard work and no wins was the Ohio way.

Around this time, subtle changes in our culture took shape. We had newer skaters who were lifelong athletes, who hadn't joined for the punk rock aesthetic or even a love of roller skating. Rather, they saw in roller derby an opportunity to play a real, competitive, full-contact sport—as adults. Something amateur park league athletics didn't offer—especially adult women's athletics.

In 2011 we qualified for a postseason tournament after a winning season record of 11–5. This would be the first time we'd qualify for the postseason since we hosted Heartland Havoc in 2007—the first year a postseason really existed. The derby community found our 16 games in one season a truly incredible feat. Most teams still played single game weekends, testing themselves in gameplay just a handful of weekends out of the year. We were doing double headers with our B-team on back-to-back days in one weekend, and in one case, a triple-header season opener where our charter played two games, separated by mere hours.

In terms of professional sports, 16 games might not seem like that much. But those athletes are being paid, and the games they are playing are their job. Roller derby athletes playing an internationally competitive sport is something else entirely. We shudder when people call it a "hobby" because it feels so much more than that, something we do in addition to our jobs. We pay to travel and equip ourselves, and we take time off from our jobs to go play the game. In that light, 16 games is a ton. You're giving up about a quarter of your weekends in a year for games, not to mention the mountain of preparation those games require.

But we are Ohio, underdogs forever, and we refused to find ourselves remarkable, instead preferring to just keep doing what we were doing. Or maybe even doing more of it. So, in 2012, we played a record-breaking 21 regular season games. We won 20 of them, losing only to Carolina Roller Derby (Raleigh, North Carolina) by 15 points in April. We had T-shirts printed up with our opponents on the back like a touring rock band—and we included the scores. This was the closest we had ever come to exuding confidence. We were actually acknowledging what we were achieving. It was almost boasting.

My confidence extended as far as to inviting my parents to come to our postseason tournament in August 2012. I felt like it could be our year, and while they'd been coming to watch us play since our first season, they'd never been to a tournament. The trip to Niagara Falls wasn't all that far from Columbus, and since I figured there would be plenty for them to do when not watching us play, I brought it up.

Around the same time, my grandfather's health began failing. In his 80s, he still biked several times a week, but his cardiologist recommended he take a break, even a vacation. So not only did my parents make the trip, so did my grandparents, and my aunt and uncle. My aunt made the family "derby derbies" by trimming black felt derby hats with green ribbons.

We came into that tournament seeded sixth. At the end of the weekend, the top three teams would advance to world championships. We weren't overtly talking about it very much, but it did feel like that feat was in the realm of possibility for the first time ever. But even with our recent confidence, we couldn't admit to ourselves that it was at all realistic.

On Friday, we faced Arch Rival Roller Derby (St. Louis, Missouri), and we beat them, which advanced us to semifinals and a game against Windy City, whom we had never beaten in all the times we'd faced them. We played Windy on Saturday, and while the game was close for much of the time, we fell short. This still left us in a good position, and in totally new territory, as it sent us into the third-place game in the final round. Winning would mean not only bronze medals hanging from our necks, but more games that year at championships.

After gearing down postgame versus Windy, I checked my Facebook account in the locker room. I was utterly confused to find several people home in Columbus posting on my wall—not about our performance, but about how cute my grandpa was. I left the locker room and found fellow WFTDA board member Grace Killy chatting with my parents. All the parts of my life were converging.

The derby derbies had attracted some attention in the crowd, and unbeknownst to me, while we were strategizing in the locker room at half-time, Erica "Double H" Vanstone, then the WFTDA broadcast director, had asked if she could interview my grandparents about their hats on the WFTDA.tv livestream. My grandmother begged off, but my mom joined Grandpa on camera with Erica. The video is still on YouTube, and I watch it periodically to see the look on Erica's face as my grandfather proudly proclaims that he met my grandmother at the roller rink. She later excitedly told me that she was not expecting him to say that, and I had to tell her that I hadn't either, as I was totally unaware of it until this point. They'd come to my games for six years and watched me skate since I was little, and neither he nor my grandmother ever thought to mention this.[8]

Despite us unexpectedly ending up with a Sunday game, my family decided the weekend had been long enough at this point and wished us well before starting the trip back to Ohio. Maybe those derby derbies had been our good luck charm, because once they were out of the building, we lost our footing. In our final game, we had several injuries to key players early on and ended up losing to Naptown by over 100 points. Is it possible we choked? Maybe. We hadn't thought champs was a possibility, and so being thrust into that new situation, as well as the sheer exhaustion of the year, left us on the losing side. Still, we left that tournament in fourth place. The tournament MVP blocker (Phoenix Bunz) and jammer (The Smacktivist) were both on our team. And we had had a taste of what it felt like to play at that level. Now we could truly plan for a real run at champs.

In November, we watched the championships tournament online, and we thought about what could have been and what could still be. My grandfather entered the hospital, and I got pulled away from practices and team stuff, traveling to be with my family as his health declined. He passed away on Thanksgiving weekend, followed by my uncle on Christmas Eve. It was an incredibly stressful time of my life, and I didn't even realize until a couple of years later that it just so happened to occur while we were on our off-season break—as if real life was only allowed to happen when derby was done.

I took the break and mourned during the holidays. Then I went back to roller derby again in January—to all of it.

---

8   Both my grandparents have since passed away, and their skates are proudly displayed in my house, all worn white leather and wooden wheels.

5 Pivot

In those fleeting three months as a wannabe athlete, the most important thing I learned was: one does not dominate roller derby; roller derby dominates you.

Athletics never came naturally to me but neither did admitting defeat. A proud dummy, I walked off the back pain as I walked off the team, claiming my leave was purely circumstantial. Since I was already lying to myself, I further explained to my three fans that my 2010 Pikes Peak Derby Dames retirement had nothing to do with my growing list of physical ailments; it was simply "time to retire" and "move on to different things." This also allowed me to ignore critical examinations of my impulse to join in the first place, and to pretend I was suffering even greater heartbreak about losing the one thing that had nearly saved me from my grief.

The timing of the knee tear and the back break and the shame-faced bullshitting happened to align with the other hobby I'd quietly attended all year: getting the hell out of America. Jesse and I, with our heaping amounts of underemployment, decided living abroad might solve all our problems.[1] We saw leaving as a last attempt to get back on track of the American Dream, or at least a reprieve from the empty promise of it.

Jesse and I were on the verge of applying for Medicaid, a need I'd been dodging—then sidestepping as I still could not bend—for

---

1   Yes, I'm noting the pattern as well. Things get tough, and Sam skates off at breakneck speed.

months. If we moved to South Korea instead, we'd have stable incomes, more work opportunities than we could keep up with, a paid for and furnished apartment—and health insurance. Truly, somehow, it made more sense to me to live internationally than to apply for Medicaid, as my various jobs refused to cover me. I wasn't sure I deserved Medicaid coverage. *I* had made the choice to play a full-contact sport.

Listen to variations on this very American phrase once more:

> I don't know if I deserve health care.
> I'm not sure my body is worth taking care of.
> My body has to be deemed worthy to be healed (with the medical advancements that were made precisely for healing.)
> I deserve pain because I have it and I cannot pay to fix it.

Oof, right?

But this wasn't the only reason I avoided government assistance, or, as they call it in other countries, "health care." I knew my mother would be upset, perhaps even angry, if I were on the dole.[2]

In fact, my siblings and I had been on Medicaid until our late teens, a necessity and a lifesaver for my family. I remember Mom hurrying us from school event to school event as she worked full-time at Walmart and juggled college. She hustled to better our lives and supplement spotty child support payments. She did it so one day her own children wouldn't have to struggle in the same way. I think my mom saw my adult financial struggles as commentary on her own struggle. As if she failed because I suffered the same issues she had suffered—but inexplicable to her, as I had a college degree, no children, and a spouse who was present and sober.

Mom, however, could not have accounted for student loans, unmanageable rents, economic crises, war-ravaged loss, mental health fallout, subsequent random attempts at brutal team sports, lack of health care, rinse, repeat. And I didn't know how to tell her I was doing the best I could or that I was starting to suspect our country is broken. That our country chooses to punish rather than help those who lack. That we shouldn't internalize it, shouldn't feel ashamed about being in need. I wished to explain, "Hey Mom, we started from the bottom and now we're here, but it's only, like, a tiny bit higher from the bottom and it's got nothing to do with your invaluable efforts."

---

2   Most things sound more manageable in Britishisms.

I felt deeply ashamed, as if I'd let my mom down and that I'd brought the whole drama on myself. Even if I was in the depths of grief, there is no place in poverty for bad decision-making, no excuse for wanting to do things that people with health insurance and steady pay and a lust for life do. If I was going to play a difficult, risky sport on a whim, uninsured, because I wanted to be someone other than myself,[3] then I deserved to walk things off.

Instead, I downplayed all of my pain. I did not want to add to her own. I chose a routine of scalding baths and gel tabs, ice packs and silent tears. I visited a chiropractor with a coupon, paid 20 bucks to no avail. And then, I decided to leave America.

We left for Korea in August of 2010. I spent June and July packing, selling furniture on Craigslist, and I quit my job at the Boy Scouts. My boss was surprisingly impressed by the "whole roller derby thing" and though he did not mention his feelings about my *Kegel Scout*–ing, he did tell me a full-time position—with health insurance—had become available. After we received our passports, after the paperwork was done.

"Several months too late," I said, relieved that I would not have to take the job.

As I struggled to pack up my life or entertain the idea of any physical movement, I left my derby gear in a pile beside the dining room table. Roller derby protective gear, the soggy knee pads and helmets and skates and all, has a particular nasty smell. It is sour and aggressive and smacks of intense physical training. My little-used gear had no smell at all, unless the stench of failure counts. Every time I looked at the gym bag, my black-and-yellow laces crisscrossing my lovely, expensive Riedell skates, I felt a sadness that, for once in a long time, had nothing to do with the loss of Ronnie. After a bit, I welcomed this new pain. It was surprising that one sadness might offer relief of another sadness, but that's what happened. I was heading back out into the world, which made me vulnerable to new things. Turns out that's what I had needed. I still had to live.

I would make roller derby a memory, a momentary lapse of reason, and flee to Korea to win at something different. My husband and I put our lives into storage. I put my brother and war there, too, set both down and pretended they wouldn't be waiting for me upon return. I buried my skates and gear in a blue duffle bag, behind our microwave

---

3   Studies show grieving, grief, et al. is often eased by routine physical activity and community making.

and bikes and sofas, like evidence I'd need later, proof I'd once (dreadfully) done a remarkable thing in the face of so much grief.

In Korea,[4] the doctor diagnosed a PCL tear in my left knee. The knee hurt did not ease for months, and my back pain did, so I ordered their importance accordingly. Then the back pain subsided enough for me to try and forget about it. Even with affordable health insurance, I only addressed the most pressing issues, learned behavior after a lifetime of costly health care instabilities. I could have gotten X-rays or physical therapy, or made sure my back wasn't broken,[5] but the thought was too scary to consider. The pain lessened, the doctor prescribed six months of light to no physical activity, and I became absorbed by my new life abroad. I taught English on a giant tour bus turned classroom called "the Magic English Bus!" The seat benches had been taken out, the entire bus gutted, retrofitted with a small, preschooler-sized table and a five-foot-tall magnet board map and a library of children's books to be accompanied by baskets of hand puppets. We traveled to new elementary schools every few days, my two Korean co-teachers and a giant blond British man and a small bus driver I was told to call Driver. Life was a blur of excitable children and intense, close but volatile relationships, the kind that are forged when people are trapped on a bus together for six hours, every day, for a year. My red hair soaked up the Busan humidity, my new identity as Ms. Frizzle complete.

Well into our first year in Korea, my husband heard from a fellow expat that there was a roller derby team in Daegu. A few towns away from our home in Busan, Daegu had an American military base, and several Americans there had started a league. We'd visited other English teaching friends there once, on Thanksgiving, desperate for the turkey feast that American-adjacent folks could provide. Roller derby's international presence grew exponentially during our Korea years, and before long, I heard another team had been founded in Seoul.

Of course, I'd immediately told my new international friends about roller derby. It was such an easy conversation starter, a catchall for everything I hoped to represent to potential new friends: I'm tough and

---

4   It's called universal health care—you might wanna look it up.

5   It was, you fool! It was.

cool and worthy, so worthy. Most of our new friends were from the UK or Australia or New Zealand, and I wanted to stand out—I did not want to be pegged as *one of those* Americans—so I behaved, ironically, in the most American way possible. I made my politics known early and often. I offered my brother's death as explanation for my (very new and) not fleshed out radical leftist ideas. I bragged about my grandmother—my *halmoni*—and my Korean heritage, though my White face undermined it all. I mentioned roller derby play casually in conversation, hoping my direct if vague insights of the sport implied a vast but complex knowledge rather than a glancing and uncritical understanding.[6]

Word got out about the new leagues, and my new international friends seemed thrilled at the chance to watch me skate and hit and fall. I made excuses about how far I'd have to travel to get to practice, an hour one way, and then someone suggested I start my own league in Busan. I hedged for a time, then announced my mother refused to send my gear through the mail because of the cost—the shipping, the shipping insurance, could all amount to upwards of $500. This was an arbitrary number I pulled out of my butt. I never asked Mom to send any of it. I was not honest with anyone, not even myself, about how freaked I was at the idea of returning to skates.

While I began publicly distancing myself from the sport to avoid joining again, I Facebook-stalked my ex-teammates. The Swiss Missile transferred to Denver, one of the top-five teams in the country. My friend Koko, the only Black roller derby player I'd ever met, a skater who'd made the team at the same time I did, eventually transferred to Atlanta—an extremely successful and talented team in WFTDA.

The longer I quietly kept up with them and their successes, the more I realized that somewhere along the way I'd truly fallen in love with roller derby. Maybe it started as a distraction or an attempt at finding myself in the depths of grief, but it had grown beyond this. I had been consumed with my brother, who he had been, and who he would never get to be. I did need distraction from the loss, but I'd also convinced myself to live an extraordinary life to make up for the time he was denied. I wanted do things he'd appreciate, maybe even be proud of. In Korea, I gained enough space and distance to analyze my attempt at amateur athleticism. But when I thought about the material cost, well over $1,000 in gear and dues, the emotional and physical cost too,

---

6   Wait a second . . . am I the America of people?

I berated myself. I decided I deserved what would likely amount to life-long back and knee pain for being impulsive. I had no right to be proud of an attempt at greatness when the result was one of abject failure.

I've never been great at giving myself a break.[7]

Roller derby was the first time in my life I did physical activity for joy and function, and not for weight loss. When I was athletic-adjacent as a teen, a.k.a. speed walking with my mother and sister, it was because I was taught the best way to look was exactly like Britney Spears.[8] I should have also been taught that Britney[9] *is* an athlete, a dancer, a professional. The demand of her performances necessitated daily hours in the gym, in a dance studio, in a pool, or on the yoga mat. All I had as a wide-hipped, massively assed, flat-chested '90s teen was TV and glossy mags, all *Glamour*, no context. I tried grapefruit diets and sucked in my stomach at all times and waited for my body to arrive. It never occurred to me how hard-won Britney's body was. My culture set me up to either look like her or resent her when I certainly could not look remotely like her.

It was early, when I stopped regarding my body in a positive, kind way—or had I ever begun? As young as 12 I did 50 sit-ups a day, determined to stop flesh drifting over the lip of my JNCO jeans. I memorized mantras like "Nothing tastes as good as thin feels" or "Eat to live, don't live to eat!" My friends and I power walked the mall on Friday nights, sucking in our guts and clenching our butt cheeks like we were stashing cash up there. We didn't have *any* cash, just a lot of time on our hands and new teenage hormones insisting we had grown out of our Skate City phases.

Every woman I know—and most men, surely, though not as openly—has suffered a similar general dysfunction in eating and exercise habits. It is so commonplace, the disordered care of our bodies, that I did not recognize how much it began to rule my life in Korea, mostly because I had, once again, failed to critically assess what I had been through: I broke my body at Riot Grrrl Disneyland, sure, but I'd also gained muscle and connected to my physical self in new ways; I

---

7   Except for that one time I broke my back. Ha!

8   A Word from Amy Spears: No relation.

9   Britney would kill in roller derby. She'd make an excellent jammer. She'd dance through packs, leap lines with a gymnast's grace.

had a very good time for three months straight and met some fascinating and mostly kind people, despite my monstrous grief.

It took me years to reframe the experience this way. Instead of internalizing the realization that roller derby as exercise was excellent for my mental and physical health, I focused on the weight I had lost (and would certainly regain). The whole experience converted into numbers on a scale. I was less afraid of losing mobility due to injury than I was terrified I may not be able to run off potential pounds. By the time my Korean physical therapist cleared me for exercise, I'd already started hiking every day, lifting weights, squatting at potties and everywhere else in Busan. I stopped intensive exercise for all of six weeks, not the recommended six months. I refused to gain back the weight I'd lost playing roller derby. I convinced myself thinness was the only thing I had achieved in the experience.

During my short derby stint, I'd run 5Ks and lifted weights and stood at the front of kickboxing classes. I felt so good, physically, that I wanted to exercise as close to the instructor as possible. Yes, okay, I wanted to win kickboxing class. I wanted, needed, to win everything. I was always competitive; at this time in my life, however, I'd reached new, obscene levels of wanting to win. I was searching for something like control.

Because I had more free time in Korea, I began exercising 90 minutes a day, six or seven days a week. I was running without losing my breath, I was obsessed with daily high-intensity workouts, and I was eating incredible, fresh, healthy Korean food. My second year in Korea, I left the Magic English Bus for an all-girls high school at the top of a steep hill. I scaled it each day with little effort. I hiked the mountain behind my apartment building several times a week. I was winning at exercise.

And then I won at feeling cold all the time. I won at having to buy a whole new wardrobe, won when Korean clothing store clerks stopped insisting I was "large size." For the first time in my life my hip bones protruded, and I started grabbing at them several times a day, holding on like they owed me money. Prior to Korea, I was covered in hip level bruises, that part of my body weaponized on the track, but now the hip bruises were a result of being far too thin and running into tables. The weight loss, around 35 pounds total, also altered my balance and coordination. I certainly couldn't dance as well with a daintier ass. With my body at a new Korean size, "Gangnam Style" was as good as I got, giddy-up. My previously thicc[10] moves were modeled after Rihanna,

---

10   Curvy, full-bodied, bangin'.

not horse girls, but my body had become unrecognizable. I relished my sudden waifish physique.

Korea will always be one of the most important times and places of my life. I learned so much about my family, my beliefs, my politics, myself. Much of the importance, however, is in the accumulation of past pain, my physical and mental injuries. When I did not take time to recognize these traumas, I brought the resulting dysmorphia back home with me. We spent two years in Korea, then moved back to Colorado in 2012 for my first round of graduate school. I had never been so thin, so small and diminished, in my life.

I did not transition well back to life in America. I had a panic attack in a grocery store, immobilized by so much choice, the rows and rows of pretty packaged cookies. I didn't even want cookies, but I'd lost all access to them in Korea, so I stayed in the aisle trying to make a choice I didn't need to make. I kept trying to exercise as I had in Korea, not understanding that it

1. was an illogical and frankly unhealthy amount of exercise that
2. was no longer possible in a grueling grad school setting.

I once said that Ohio is the America of America—a persevering place *despite* (we're at the place in the book where I begin quoting myself as an expert in something I said earlier). That word, *despite*, has always been key. It is so applicable to how I've considered who I am throughout much of my life. Poor, but persevering. Injured, but impervious. Grief stricken, going on. It can't be a coincidence that someday I'd play for a roller derby team in Ohio that runs on Despite with a capital *D*—overachievers forever fighting against a lingering underdog reputation. But when and why did I conflate overcoming obstacles with winning everything, with winning at life? How does one even go about winning at life? And how did this urge to overcome a tough childhood, my brother's death, a broken back, turn into an eating disorder?[11]

I've found the problem with feeling forever like an underdog, like an impostor, is that there is never enough. Believing I was an underdog

---

11 We can call it disordered eating, food obsession, overexercise. We can dance around what's really going on with way too many of us, but perhaps instead if we just admit American culture promotes eating disorders, then we can address our mental and physical well-being and get on with our lives.

convinced me I could and should win at life—which, in my experience, impedes my living of life. I'm not suggesting this attitude, this perspective, is always more dangerous than motivating, and I'll admit, wanting more and more and more has led me to fascinating places. But winnings aren't wins when you operate from a place of Despite. They are more like happy accidents, unrelated to the real mental and emotional and physical labor we put in prior to said happy accident. When I deployed my Despite logic alongside my perfectionist impulses, I ended up hurting myself so much more than I'd been hurt in the first place. When I held my body to the same unreasonable standard—because of cultural influence, deep insecurity, or an incapability of honoring my body as is—I further damaged my body.

After South Korea, back in Colorado, I woke up earlier and earlier to make time for exercise before grad classes. I trained for and ran a half-marathon, along with spin sessions and weight lifting and P90X, and my back started hurting again. My knees popped like chewing gum and ached in winter, but I refused to quit running. I never stopped thinking about food, what I should or should not be eating. I still casually mentioned my roller derby playtime in unrelated conversations, though less often—it felt like a thing of the past now. My body was a different body. I was slim and that seemed to speak for itself. People flirted with me in overt ways. Women asked how I did it. My mom, who knew me well enough to be concerned, said, "Sam—you look gaunt. What's up?"

I finished my master's at Colorado State, and the MFA at The Ohio State University called. We were destined for Ohio. We packed what we had only just unpacked. As I rifled through another closet full of half-opened boxes, I came across my skates and I smiled. I was holding a small fortune in my hands, and it was time I got my money's worth.

I took them, a Nalgene water bottle, and several ibuprofen to the local rink. Rollerland Fort Collins is like the rest of them, the Skate Cities and Worlds and Galaxies, places of easy fun and instant, uncomplicated nostalgia. As I tied my laces, I felt more content than I had in a long time. I slid out. My back and knees did not ache the way they did when I ran. I relaxed and moved with the music and realized I was, for the first time since the last time I'd worn my beloved skates, not forcing myself to exercise. I was in my body, mindful, present, having fun.

I was lost in memories of my old skate rinks and being a kid, thinking about how often I'd fallen and fought my way back up, when "Gangnam Style" came over the speakers. Kids at the Colorado rink lost their minds. They screamed and horse jumped on skates, waved their hands high and low as they howled a garbled Korean. I sped around, through the American children, laughing so hard I cried.

Life is difficult, and people roller skate.

We arrived in Ohio on August 1, 2014, and my back had throbbed through the cross-country Penske drive. My graduate school health insurance would be through The Ohio State University, so I made an immediate appointment, and by October I had met a doctor, gone for X-rays, and came back for a diagnosis.

My doc was excellent and took extensive notes during each visit as I recalled how my back pain came and went, the way it worsened when I ran or sat and graded papers for hours at a time. She said she did not expect any major issues, but the day the X-rays came in, she sat me down and asked, "When did you break your vertebrae? Why didn't you mention this?"

"Wait, what?"

"You clearly broke endplates here," she said, pointing to what she called the L3 and L4. "The breaks would have been a number of years ago, as they are already healed. The issues you have now are arthritic."

For a moment I couldn't say anything. Then I realized after so many years of bragging about my "career" in roller derby, I had not mentioned it to the doctor. I had not gone that far back in my medical history because I no longer connected the back pain to the time and place it began. I saw it as an infrequent nuisance, chalked it up to aging or pinched nerves. I had ignored it off and on for almost five years. At this point, I thought of it as a series of injuries, not one long, plaguing issue—all of this another example of me, always trying to overcome, always trying.

"Well, I guess this probably happened around five years ago, when I didn't have health insurance. I used to play roller derby," I said to the doctor.

She sucked her teeth. She shook her head and looked like my mother as she asked, "Now, why would you do a thing like that?"

Kristi "Phoenix Bunz" Burress
(Credit: Rachel Turner)

OHIO PLAYER PROFILE: THE MASTERMIND

I didn't know it was one of my life's goals to be sculpted in fondant until I was standing in front of the cake at Phoenix Bunz and Great Scott's wedding. It was three tiers, elegant and traditional, until you got to the topper. No plastic bride and groom here; instead, the decorator had re-created one of the photos from their engagement shoot: Bunz in her roller derby uniform, lime-green fishnets, and one skate in the air, arms around the neck of Scott in his referee uniform and skates.

Her butt even looked good when made out of sugar paste.

The wedding had a large contingent of derby folks in attendance. Prior to the ceremony, a whole row of attendees discovered we were wearing black athletic shorts under our fancy dresses (because roller derby thighs chafe, after all). Both Bunz and Scott had been involved since the early days of OHRD, having joined when we still had home teams. They'd both seen all the growing pains, filling all sorts of roles within our league from board member to head coach of a team that went to world champs. At the time, Bunz's day job was as an actuary for one of the major insurance companies here in Columbus. She used those financial skills as treasurer for several years, advising the rest of the board on when we were risking too much. Ultimately, she formulated the plan to get us out of our early startup debt.

When Bunz started with OHRD, she was drafted to one of our home teams, The Sprockettes, the home team that could not catch a break. They had been plagued by injuries and retirements for the entirety of their existence and they won a few games over three years. Had we gone one more season with home teams, I have no doubt Bunz would have pulled them to the top of the ranks through leadership and pure athleticism. And skating in a purple tutu, no less.

Having lettered in three sports in college, Bunz was part of the new guard when she joined OHRD. An athlete first and skater second, an early coach once stated that she skated "like a caveman" due to her wide stance. We looked to see if she would utterly eviscerate him, but she just smiled, even when we made Captain Caveman signs for her at the postseason tournament later that year. She is an incredibly serious person, but not one who can't take (or make) a joke at her own expense. She was known for being able to focus through weeks of practice and games, then flip the switch to let her hair down and enjoy cherry vodka sodas at the after-party, once the work was done.

At some point, Bunz earned the nickname "Derby-Bot 3000" because never has there been another player who we have so much suspected was a robot, purely due to her endurance. By her final season, the team had her playing every position, sometimes back to back. Announcers noted when she was *not* on the track for Ohio, because that was an anomaly. At the end of our first game at WFTDA Championships in 2013 versus Rat City, she jammed back to back an unprecedented three times, finally cementing the win not on physical but mental endurance as she smartly ran out the game clock while the opposing jammer was in the penalty box. It seems fitting that one of the few times she got to rest during that tournament she was still on the track, anxiously skating back and forth out of range of the pack, luckily right in front of our fan base, eyes locked to the clock hovering over the center of the track, until she was able to tap her hips to end the jam, the game, and earn one more last game for her team. Which would also be the last of her roller derby career with OHRD. The long whistle blew, and the switch flipped—business Bunz became celebratory as the rest of us on the track skated back to hug her.

Bunz is a planner, a goal setter, a goal achiever. We knew it was her last season, we knew something big was coming after all the games were over, so when she and Scott announced they were selling their condo and moving to Hawaii, we were surprised but not at all shocked. They had a plan, they stuck to it, they did it. And they kept at it. They live in Seattle now, and they have two kids—Jett and Revv—who appear to have inherited their mother's sense of athleticism. She did, after all, teach a fitness class the day she gave birth to Jett. (Again, we suspect she may be a robot.)

She may have moved on from OHRD, from Columbus, from Ohio, from roller derby, but her legacy will forever remain. Her number, 23—originally given to her by a childhood coach—has been retired, and telling that story lets us impart a bit of her spirit on to newer members who came long after.

—Amy Spears

A Word from Amy Spears, Married, Divorced, Remarried to Roller Derby

For every bit that roller derby saved me, it broke me just as much.

Some people have spouses. I have roller derby. Some people have children. I have roller derby. Some people have skyrocketing careers. I have roller derby.

This is not to say I feel like I have roller derby at the expense of any of those things. Roller derby is the thing I very consciously chose. I have always been a collector of hobbies. I remember once writing on a bio sheet "I collect everything but dust." And it's true, I do a lot of things. I have hobbies to distract myself from my hobbies. At some point, I know I felt a sort of guilt or failing over the fact that I'd spend a few years on one and then move on to the next. Moderation is not something I understand or enjoy very much when it comes to learning how to do stuff, and then doing it.

I never really decided how long I'd skate. At the very beginning, I remember having conflicting thoughts. On one hand, I told myself I'd be out of it before I ended up responsible for anything. On the other, if I did it for a little bit and then moved on, it would feel as if I'd added roller derby to a long list of things I'd checked off on my list, but didn't so much finish as do for a while and then leave behind.

About 5 years in, I do recall thinking that it might be nice to set a goal of playing for 10 years. No one knew how long the "average" derby career was, and it seemed to me like longevity could be the way I carved out my niche. On doing the math, I realized that just playing one year beyond that would mean I'd play until I turned 40, which felt like a nice round number. So that became the default goal; play until 40, then reevaluate. I turned 30 at the end of our first season, and I spent the entirety of that decade of my life in a sport and subculture that hadn't existed a few years before I began.

The year we made it to world champs was season eight for me. By this point I'd seen enough teammates come and go that we'd all talked about when we might retire. No one ever wanted to become irrelevant. But to go out right on top felt like too abrupt an exit too. I knew I didn't want to find myself surpassed by newer players and still be hanging on, like some sort of Al Bundy–esque character reliving his high school football glory days. But I still felt good, and I was still immersed in everything OHRD and WFTDA. So the 10-year goal cemented in a little stronger. I wasn't going anywhere.

It's possible I felt a little more pressure to keep going that season than I had in the past. We had a team meeting early on that year and explicitly decided that getting to champs was a goal that year. We wrote it down. And we also had two players announce that it would be their final season. Our captain, Phoenix Bunz—quite possibly one of the best athletes our sport, let alone our team, has ever seen—made it explicit that she would do everything in her power to get us to champs, but that this was the last season for her. Then there was Pippi RipYourStockings. Pippi started months before me and was one of a handful of players who had been around since our very first season. She was my first captain, responsible for drafting me to a home team. She had a reputation for being an intense person on and off the track. Announcers liked to joke that for cross-training, Pippi chopped wood. It was funny because it was true—Pippi totally did this. But 10 years of a contact sport had taken a toll on her and she was facing the need for surgery on both her knees. She felt she could give it one more year.

Both of our coaches were also going to be moving on. Great Scott, a high-level certified referee, was now our head coach. He and Bunz had gotten married the year prior, and they had plans for their lives beyond roller derby. BFF, who had been with us for a few years on the bench, also had this one last season in her plans.

This was a new thing for us—to know that players would be moving on before it happened. To have people intentionally planning things out. It was refreshing to see people making conscious decisions to move on rather than having their derby careers ended by injuries. People sometimes had major life changes in their jobs or family life and kept skating, only later realizing it wasn't sustainable, leaving midseason. It was one of the first times we felt like we knew the stakes going into the season, but those stakes were higher than they'd ever been.

Leading that early meeting, Bunz made it clear: we could do this, and we would do this, but only if we all bought in. This was going to be intense. It was going to be hard. And it wasn't going to work if everyone wasn't on board. We had to commit to a set of priorities: (1) Family, (2) Work, (3) Roller Derby. We all did.

And so once again, we embarked on playing a huge season. We played 20 regular season games with a record of 15–5. The losses were, in our minds, "good losses"—a phrase we wouldn't have thought existed a few years prior. We lost to Arch Rival, who we'd beaten at the prior year's playoffs, with a short roster in their home venue. We lost narrow games to Atlanta and Philly, both ranked in the top 10 to our top 20. We beat the team who served us our only loss in 2012's regular season, when Carolina came to Columbus and we won by triple digits.

We were confident but realistic. When we doubted ourselves, we threw ourselves into training and cross-training. I've always said and known that roller derby is a huge part of my life, but that particular year, it was basically all of my life. Any moment not at work was 100 percent for derby. It was welcome as a distraction from the grief that ended 2012 for me from deaths in my family and the end of a relationship. It let me throw myself into something rather than dwelling on loss. This was, after all, what had gotten me into derby in the first place. Of course, this was the plan.

It was also around this time that we felt the opposite side of what success can feel like. For years, we'd had the underdog reputation and found fans at tournaments when we demonstrated that storyline, coming in underranked and not expected to do much, then winning games without a lot of flash, playing a game focused on strategy and endurance. We flourished in that light, probably because it allowed us to be confident without having to give up the humility that had always underscored the way we felt about our team. But this year, when our win-loss record stood out so much, we started to hear more critical comments in the derby media. A website that offered commentary and predictions for games coming up the next weekend consistently picked against us. They would ignore the fact that we'd been on a streak, that we'd had a consistent roster of players who had been playing together for 5–10 years in some cases, and then would express "surprise" the following weekend when we were victorious.

To this day, I don't think any of this was intentional. The very fact that "derby media" was the only media covering our sport, and the fact that volunteers couldn't be everywhere at once and that internet streaming of games was still pretty sporadic, meant in many cases they didn't know a lot about us. So for that reason, our success was probably honestly surprising to them. Week after week, we continued with our plan, and they continued with their surprise. It began to be an inside joke with us. Despite that, our rankings rose and all things were going as we'd intended, and after the June 30, 2013, cutoff, we patiently waited for our postseason tournament assignment.

The postseason brackets were released and we came into the Fort Wayne, Indiana, playoff tournament as the sixth seed, facing the third seed in the first round. That third seed? Arch Rival—the same opponent we'd faced in our first playoff game the year before.

This in itself was a situation racked with emotion. It wasn't just that we'd be playing the same opponent we beat in our first playoff game the prior year, or that they'd beaten us solidly in the regular season this year. It was also that Arch Rival's team name was so apt, particularly for us. Our relationship has pretty much always been the definition of friendly rivalry. We play fierce games on the track, and when we are done, we actually go to the after-party and hang out—it's not lip service.

And then there's Chewblocka. Chewie started her derby career with Arch Rival in 2006. Before even playing a game there, her husband's job was transferred to Columbus, and she joined our league, though she didn't see gameplay until the next year, being that transfers weren't a thing anyone had thought of yet. After that, she was a solid player on both our home team The Take-Outs and the OHRD charter team. But in 2011, Mr. Chewie had gotten transferred back to St. Louis, and so Chewie transferred back to her original team. In both those playoff tournaments, we were playing against our friend and former teammate. This was fun, but also hard. She knew us and we knew her—both on track and off. In a single elimination tournament, one loss means you don't move on, so it was her or us. Arch Rival was ranked and seeded above us, so we had to win.

When that tournament came around in Fort Wayne that September, we pulled off the upset. While our win over Arch in 2012 had been by a slim 10-point margin, we upped the ante at this tournament and won 218–166. And with that, we'd sealed the fate of both teams, knocking Arch out of contention and finalizing our spot in the top-four finishers. The top three would go to champs.

Our second opponent that weekend was Montreal Roller Derby's New Skids on the Block. We'd met previously—notably in the second-ever international roller derby game—when we beat them by four points at ECDX in 2009. But the difference between 2009 roller derby and 2013 roller derby from a strategy perspective was enormous. Montreal had risen even more sharply in the rankings than we had in that time, and they came into this tournament seeded second.

Winning the Montreal game would mean a definite trip to championships. Losing would mean a second chance to get there, but we'd have to beat either Denver or London. Of the three, we were most confident against Montreal, a team of players similar in physical stature to us, and we were happy the seeding worked out this way. At the end of that Saturday game, we'd come out on top 212–149. We were for sure going to champs in November, in Milwaukee, in one of our favorite venues to skate in. We had done it, for Pippi and for Bunz and for all of us.

We still had one more game to play for seeding, against Denver on Sunday. We weren't at all confident against Denver, who had plenty of experience fighting for champs seeding out of playoffs and who had a reputation for strategic play. We lost that game—a big loss—but we were still going to champs, and we were a second seed. We left Fort Wayne with silver medals and about six weeks to prepare for the end of our season. And we left with a brand-new goal: to be one of the select few teams who would win a game at champs in their first time competing there.

All of WFTDA's postseason tournaments are single elimination brackets. Due to the expenses of travel, playoff tournaments have consolation brackets in order to make sure teams don't make a major trip to play one game. But champs is one-and-done. If you lose, your tournament weekend is over, so winning a game at that level would be huge. Again, we had to hold our breath until the seeding was announced. Coming out of our playoff in second place meant we would face another playoff's third-place team—for once, it was possible we had a competitive seeding advantage! But our playoff was the first one played, so we had a long time to wait as the other three playoffs took place during the following month. Meanwhile, we filled in speculative brackets as another set of advancing teams was determined each successive weekend.

Seeding for champs was announced one evening when we didn't have practice, and immediately, the text messages started flying. We would face Rat City Rollergirls (Seattle) in our first game, a team we'd never played, and a team I'd always wanted to face on the track. Another original WFTDA league. One of the few who also had green as their team color.

And then we read further in the bracket. While losing to Rat City would mean the end of our season, winning would mean one more game, against a playoff-winning team, a top seed. One more game to add to our season record. One more time to hit the track with Bunz and Pippi. And that game would be against Gotham Roller Derby from New York City—the reigning world champs.

Not just the reigning champs, Gotham was the only team to have repeated that feat, and by this point, they had not lost a single game in three years. And they only played the best of the best.

Our work was cut out for us, that was clear from the start, but what we didn't necessarily expect was having to continue to work against the perception of our team off the track in the larger derby community. People were still incredulous that we had qualified for champs. Pre-tourney articles and even in-game announcers during the tournament continually referred to us as a third-place team even though we had come in second at our playoff. The assumption was made that we were on the bottom. Whether it was because it was our first champs run, or because that early perception of Ohio as a losing team was still there, or simply because we were continuing to be overlooked, I don't know. At first we kind of found it funny, but it did wear on us after a while. There were times we were referred to as a "relatively new team," which perplexed us, because not only had we been around since the beginning of WFTDA, but the core players of our team had played together for nearly a decade. Every player on the team had played 30–40 games in the past two years—more than some higher-ranked teams had played in twice that time. We were not new to roller derby. In fact, we arguably had more experience than anyone, yet the perception continued.

Perhaps the sentiment that was most hurtful was the one that presumed the only reason we'd gotten to champs at all was that we'd had such advantageous seeding at playoffs. And true, we reaped the benefit of facing opponents well known to us. But it wasn't like Arch Rival or Montreal were easy to beat teams, and in fact, both of them have had multiple champs runs since that year. Sure, Denver killed us in that final playoff game, but we had already earned our spot at that point. And there are often pretty big spreads even within teams at that level. We could have been defensive about all of this, but Bunz said it best when she coolly responded to someone who voiced that another team should have made it instead of us. "Well, we won our games," she shrugged. It wasn't meant to be catty. It was simply a fact.

Champs were held in Milwaukee, and while we were still regarded as tournament newbies, or out of our element, we felt right at home.

Milwaukee's Brewcity Bruisers hosted the tournament in the same venue where they'd held their Brew Ha Ha invitational for multiple years, so it was a floor and a space well known to us. There was a comfort that also yielded confidence.

I believe that confidence, along with the enormous group of league members, friends, and family members who made the trip with us and were there cheering on turn three, led us to win that first-round game. We came out strong, caught an early lead, and completely surprised a Rat City team who had totally discounted us. In a pre-tourney interview, they talked about all the plans they'd made to face off against Gotham—ignoring that they wouldn't get to play Gotham without beating us first. That oversight was more fuel for us to take control of that game. Rat City changed strategies and staged a comeback in the second half, but it was too late. We held on and eked out a win.

Our prize? One more game. The last game for this incarnation of our team would be against Gotham.

Even though there were those who had changed their tune after our first-round win, who went into the next round cheering for Ohio after we had ruined their brackets, we went into that Gotham game knowing we were not going to win. Not in a defeatist way at all, if that's possible. The math, the history, didn't support it. Because now we were playing the team with the most experience at playing in—and winning—champs. It would have been one of the world's greatest David and Goliath sports story if we had pulled it off, but the advantageous seeding we'd enjoyed this season had come to an end.

Those of us who played that game have very different reactions to it. Some of my teammates can't bear to watch the tape even today. I have watched it multiple times. It's not a game about the outcome—it was pretty clear after a few jams no one was watching for that. It was a game of small, temporary victories. If we scored, the crowd went nuts. If we knocked a Gotham jammer out or got the better of a Gotham blocker, it was as if we'd won the whole tournament, the way the stands erupted.

It was a game played for the sake of experience. Almost every player on our roster jammed—whether or not we were jammers. (And let me tell you, spending two minutes as a non-jammer trying to pass Bonita Applebottom is on the list of hardest things I've ever done.) Everyone on the bench got playtime, whereas normally we kept our first string on the track as long as their endurance could hold. It wasn't that we weren't trying, it's that we knew winning was out of reach; it was far more important to let everyone play, get everyone time on the track against an opponent of a caliber we'd never faced rather than worry about the point differential. It was a passing of the torch, from Pippi and Bunz to the newer players: to Loraine Acid and Pearl Rogi, Ena Flash and The Smacktivist, Ava Tarr and Outa My Wayman.

The game was rough. It was not always fun. Three of us fouled out. Then it was over, along with our season.

A major era for our team was over too.

6 Mindful Jockdom

Nothing major changed after I found out my back had been broken, though I absolutely started telling people, "One time I broke my back playing roller derby." I'm nothing if not a thrilling conversationalist.

The biggest difference postdiagnosis was that I could actually attend to my injury. I used my graduate school health insurance for physical therapy, for cognitive therapy, for massage therapy, and every other kind of therapy for which I was offered coverage. The health insurance was absolutely a factor in my applying to graduate school; it became a strong reason to stay and finish, too. After two years at Colorado State and then another immediate two (going on three) at Ohio State, I'd reached peak grad school fatigue—and I still had one year to go.

By 2016, I'd had too much homework and too many papers to grade to be all-consumed with physical activity and food, and this was a positive change. My access to a nutritionist and counselors specializing in grief, disordered eating, and more (health insurance, can you believe it?) was also a game changer. These medical professionals enabled me to finally address my mental and physical health, and the undeniable connection between, in lasting ways. Nationwide, universities have begun cutting health insurance for their graduate student instructors, even as a significant number of college classes are planned, taught, and graded by said graduate students.[1] In fully funded programs like mine, grad students receive health insurance and a small stipend. Tuition and fees in fully funded programs are covered by universities, but the payoff schools get on the backs of indentured grad students far exceeds the eclectic payments offered for grad student labor. This is especially the case if schools take away health coverage. I taught many classes in the English department as I also finished my degrees, and health insurance was the biggest, most important perk of my job as a graduate teacher.

When I was ready to be the best at something other than anxiety, my university-appointed therapist and I decided I should start from scratch when it came to eating and exercise. She pushed me to embrace the effort of living mindfully. Being present was near impossible in my anxious mind, where I always worried about food, or exercise, or my body, in terms of past-present-future. If mindfulness would allow me to pay attention to the here and now, I could manage an attempt.

Perhaps I could even *win* at mindfulness.

It was in the midst of reclaiming my health when I met and fangirled all over Amy Spears. In early 2016, I told her all about my brother (killed in Iraq) before I'd even given her my name. I found out she'd retired from derby, and I told her, "Hey, we should hang out," though to be honest, neither one of us had time for that kind of commitment. My time was spent writing and grading papers and feigning meditation and subjecting my husband Jesse to Foucauldian rants about literally everything.

I was never more present and accounted for than I was at Skate Zone or United Skates, hiding from grad school altogether. On Sunday

---

1   A recently released study of public Ohio universities suggests graduate students are often more effective as instructors than full-time, tenured faculty (see Eric P. Bettinger, Bridget Terry Long, and Eric S. Taylor's article "When Inputs Are Outputs: The Case of Graduate Student Instructors" in the *Economics of Education Review*). Per a 2016 Stanford Business article on the study, "Grad-student instructors . . . help focus passionate young minds and have an outsized influence on the eventual career choice of many undergrads" (Martin J. Smith, "When Students Teach Students, the Benefits Compound").

nights, occasional Thursdays, I slung my skates over my shoulder and strapped on a cerulean blue fanny pack with a patch, proclaiming FEMINIST, sewn on. Out in the supposedly real world, it seemed as if Donald Trump might actually secure the Republican nomination for president, which really fucked with my mindfulness exercises. In the United Skates of America, I fuzzed out in the purple lights and flowed to Prince, Aaliyah, and SWV, graduate studies and panopticons be damned. The skate rinks, Columbus, became something close to home.

Columbus, Ohio, has to be made of at least 95 percent sports spectacle. Local news programming consists of Buckeye updates and football season countdowns and interviews with former players. Then the same for high school football. Commercial breaks feature car dealerships and local businesses owned by former college football celebrities. A month prior to the traditional Thanksgiving weekend game with the state up north, every *M* on every building on campus is covered with red tape *X*'s, seemingly overnight.

Even as I mocked the university and its Scarlet and Gray schtick, or worried I wasn't smart or schooled enough to be there in the first place, I didn't hesitate telling people where I was earning my free, fellowshipped MFA. Ohioans oohed and aahed like I was a fireworks display. My family started asking for sweatshirts and Buckeye gear when they realized how high profile the school is, how famous its athletic programs are, how difficult it is to get into notoriously selective MFA programs. We all agreed that my little brother would have been most thrilled about the football team, and I liked to imagine us at a game, me and Ronnie, waving at the cameras from the raucous student section, right behind The Best Damn Band in the Land.

The longer I considered, the more I saw the obsession with winning, the underdoggedness of Columbus, of Ohio, of America, and me, as a stubborn, unexamined, capitalistic, and superfluous cultural demand for competition. The feelings evoked by winning (or losing) as a part of a We are strange. The pride is contagious even as it is unwarranted. It can be community building and it can also be gross. When the Buckeyes do well, their triumphant fans cry, "We did it," though they did nothing more than scream and observe. When the Buckeyes don't win, I've seen fans react as if their brother were killed in Iraq. I have seen Buckeyes fans throw garbage cans into buildings and tend to the growing beer can gardens on their front lawns, all whether the team was winning or losing, no matter. They, the students of The Ohio State University, often flip and burn cars. The campus police watch and that is the extent of their policing in this context. Violent, sports-centric culture is allowed (for OSU students) and then allows people to be superior by association. Fandom means getting to feel a part of what we're told is a legacy. And if the team loses? Well, we were never playing with them in the first place. It's their fault. We're just the fans.

If I were feeling generous, I suppose sports wins offer reprieve from the average, uninsured, underemployed, perceived loser-led livelihood of, well, most individuals—those of us without funding, natural talent, physical prowess, or corporate sponsorship. Fortunately for someone, somewhere, Columbus is all about corporate sponsorship. For example, the Abercrombie & Fitch Emergency Department at The Ohio State University Wexner Medical Center. No joke, if my back had broken while at Ohio State, when I finally had decent health insurance, I would have received care in an emergency room paid for by Abercrombie & Fitch. This is the brand whose CEO once said, in an interview with Salon, that he did not want "fat" or "not-so-cool kids" to purchase from his clothing line. I wonder: Is the lobby of Abercrombie & Fitch Emergency poorly lit and reeking of Eau de Bro? Is there a general "no fat chicks" rule, or are they beginning to admit plus-size folks like the clothing line was forced to do after people all stopped buying their fascist collegial yuppie bullshit? As a poetry professor of mine once asked, "What's next, the Victoria's Secret Gynecological Wing?" Maybe. The owner of Victoria's Secret happens to be Les Wexner, of *The* Wexner Medical Center. Wexner is the extremely private billionaire owner of L Brands, which includes VS and Bath & Body Works and Pink, and previously the Limited, Henri Bendel, and Express. The success of early 2000s American malls and credit card debtors owe much to Wexner's empire.

Wexner attended Ohio State in the 1950s and has since cultivated an all-American, self-made hero status in Columbus, in Ohio, in the greater Midwest. Self-made is a stretch, as the Wexner family owned a clothing store during Les's adolescence, giving Les substantial means to improve upon his prior familial successes. One of the most enduring and underexamined parts of the Wexner underdog narrative is the legend of the oft-referenced $5,000 loan. A business savvy Wexner received $5,000 from an aunt in 1967. The impetus for this story seems to be that a small loan and a lot of grit will get you billionaire status. But $5,000 was not actually a small loan in 1967. The value of it today would be close to $40,000. Combined with the fact that Wexner's family owned its own business and could afford to send their son off for a college education, it's clear the only self-made thing about Wexner is the insistence that he is a self-made man. We're talking a man, Despite. A post-losing Winner. A winner who went on to build his own little Columbus-adjacent hamlet, New Albany, where rich people can roam outside of the city and avoid the poors even as they practice curated philanthropy, a.k.a. putting one's name on every building in town.

It's hard out here for a billionaire.

At its worst, Ohio is so fucking bro. It's like the Big Bro of Bro Culture. The number one Bro Goal is to always win. And in order to continue winning—whether it be via sports teams or glorified "self-made" billionaire status or walking off a broken back and emotional anguish—one has to believe they've got something to overcome. To win is to stop losing, even if losing isn't present or relevant. Living Despite is living future focused, which eliminates the context of many people's lives. It reinforces the need to overcome—to get past, to move on, to push forward—without considering present arduous or affluent circumstances. It is not mindful, and it's definitely not critical. It's American, Ohioan—it's me.

Columbus, the America of America's America, is complex in its simplicity. Here, a place whose namesake is a garbage human also has a growing brewery culture! Columbus is one of the most segregated cities in the nation, even as it is the most educated city, a prideful city even as it cultivates and improves upon the worst kind of American inequalities. Columbus is home to the most dedicated social activists I've ever met. Eventually, at some point in this book, I'll play roller derby with many of them. Columbus is average in its polarity, a decent place in desperate need of improvement, an everlasting underdog. It felt prescient, timely, to tackle my own underdog tendencies as a new Ohio American. I was ready to take stock of who and why I was, where I'd been, and how these things intertwined.

Who am I? It turns out I'm a bit of a fucking bro. I am, for all intents and purposes, a jock averse to jockdom, a competitor wholly dedicated to Despite culture, mostly in the hope of abstract greatness, of money and health and wealth, and maybe light corporate sponsorship.

And what the hell does any of this have to do with roller derby?

I know, I know, it's taken so long for me to get to Ohio Roller Derby. I'm so close.

I'm nearly there.

I'm guessing the singular, not-corporate-sponsored event in Columbus, Ohio, would be the annual Community Festival, better known as ComFest. A volunteer-run nonprofit, ComFest is held annually at Goodale Park, surrounded by gorgeous brick Victorian houses in downtown Columbus. Every late June, the park overflows with leftist political action groups, grassroots activist organizations, scheduled musicians and street performers, local artists and craftspeople, every kind of food imaginable. It is a hot, sweaty, hopeful party with a mission statement, the following listed on the homely, bare bones ComFest website:

> The Community Festival is an independent, volunteer-organized celebration of creativity and activism in Columbus, OH. Founded in 1972, its purpose is to build bridges between progressive non-profit organizations, artists, and volunteers to raise awareness and promote action within our community.
>
> Everything we do is guided by our principles which promotes community unity, tolerance, and equity.

The festival also has a Statement of Principles reinforcing their collectivist attitude, an insistence on basic needs as rights, and power to the people, billionaires not allowed.

ComFest, a hazy, happy wonder, smells like weed and patchouli or weed and heavy cologne, and sweat, so much sweat. In June 2016, it featured added layers of delirium. Trump was definitely going to win the Republican nomination. It was becoming clear he had much more than a shot at the presidency, and people wore shirts of protest, waved signs of dissent. Some women wore no shirts at all, its own kind of admirable demonstration.

ComFest felt both electrified and empty in 2016. My own graduate school bubble had burst as I noticed a growing number of neighborhood Trump lawn signs, of undergrads on campus wearing the notorious red hats. Any time I drove away from Columbus and into the Whiter suburban areas, it seemed as if he'd already won the presidency. America was fast headed to peak Bro, led there by an openly racist, pussy-grabbing, "self-made" businessman who'd made it all happen with a measly million-dollar loan from his filthy rich father. This orange guy promised to turn us from underdogs to winners. And we've long covered how Americans feel about losing, even as they're focused on winning the wrong things.

Most frustrating, I'd finally accepted I, too, was a self-loathing jock, that I was all hopped up on overcoming, ready to do anything for a metaphorical win. I was in the process of accepting myself and/or changing for the better when this hair-don't of a president came along and forced me to remember there was little place for anyone but White men in winning.

I felt so tired that day at ComFest, downtrodden and alone. My husband and I did not discuss the campaign much, even though, to me, little else felt important. He was tired of and generally uninterested in politics, and while he acknowledged his privilege in checking out, he seemed unable to recognize how that left me without support. We both had outrage fatigue. I was fatigued by feeling hopeless and outraged, and he was fatigued by my feeling hopeless and outraged. We spoke different languages. It was exhausting to be in constant translation.

Tired of men and sucking down a festival lemonade, I had finished signing a voter registration form when I noticed some badass, tattooed people walking past. They wore green-and-black shirts that said OHIO ROLLER DERBY, the O made of a weird, flaming roller skate wheel. I followed them to a tent and a table. They sold hats and crop tops, and the table had a sign-up sheet on it for anyone interested in skating. These looked like people I could share outrage fatigue with.

I approached and asked, "Is Amy Spears here?"

She was not. She was, they reminded me, retired from the team. A woman introduced herself as Outa My Wayman and asked how I knew Amy.

"Oh, we're both in the English department at OSU. I—well, I used to play roller derby. A long time ago. For a very short time."

I noticed, then, another player behind Wayman, and the tattoo on her arm, one of many across her body. I think it was Ally McSqueal. Several people on the team have this tattoo, the outline of the state of Ohio. Inside the state border tattoo it said OHIO 'TIL I DIE.

I pointed to the tat and said, "If I got that, I'd put OHIO 'TIL I MOVE."

They laughed. There's no one I love more than a person who finds me funny. If I had known them better then, we probably would have high-fived. Buncha jocks. Wayman suggested I add my name to the mailing list, in case I wanted to play rec league or see a game, and I figured I might as well. I missed skating. I missed being physical for fun, not out of fear of gaining weight. I missed being part of a group of strong, loud women. I needed community.

I'd briefly conjured a team of sorts in Korea when I accidentally started an exercise club at school. This was not with the students but with several other teachers, all women, many of whom were my English co-teachers. I taught four or five classes a day, and this left several hours open in my schedule. When I finished grading, writing, or napping in the napping room, I'd head to an empty dance studio in the basement of the school and play a kickboxing DVD. I'd return to the English office, sweaty and flushed, ready for rice cake, and after a week or so, my co-teachers wanted to know what was going on.

"You've been exercising?" Key-young asked, surprised.

Yuri said she hadn't known there was a dance studio at all. Hui-Jeong did, and added that she loved dancing. Mrs. Kim rolled her eyes, which was typical of Mrs. Kim. I invited them to join me, and we began teacher group fitness in the afternoons. Our ages ranged from almost 30 to nearing 60, and we encouraged each other to kick higher and punch harder in between our abdominal sets, which consisted of cracking each other up by mocking the school principal. I looked forward to our sessions, which felt less like a chore and more like a joyous hobby with friends.

A late-May afternoon, near the end of my time in Korea, we gathered outside in the schoolyard. The entire school faced the dirt lot, usually empty but for a few loitering girls. At all-boys' schools, the lots are in constant use, soccer games always beginning and ending. At all-girls' schools, the lots held nothing but potential. We must have been a sight, five of us stretching in full Korean outdoor apparel—wide-brimmed hats and long sleeves to protect from the sun, even as the temps and humidity broke records. Then several more women, math and history and science teachers who always smiled at me but were too shy to attempt conversation, joined us as we made laps around the yard. We alternated between jogging and running and power walking, and around 20 minutes in we heard shouts coming from the school.

Four floors of windows overlooked our exercise group, near 15 windows per floor, and our students leaned out most of them, yelling, clapping, cheering us on. Several girls leaned out and hollered, "But why, Teacher? Why, Sam, why are you doing this?"

"Because it's fun," I shouted back, keeping pace with the teachers. It was true. I was having fun. With an audience, we grew proud and picked up our speed.

Before they had to close the windows and return to studying, the girls began chanting, "Fighting! Fighting!" This is Korean English slang, or Konglish, and it's the ultimate encouragement, motivation to keep trying, keep going, don't stop, don't give up. It's a chant that's not about winning, more like—finding hope.

Lora Outa My Wayman emailed me in July 2016. By August, I'd convinced myself to drop into OHRD for a practice, if only to see what had changed in the sport of roller derby.

No pressure.

And I'd have health insurance this time.

Fighting.

OHIO PLAYER PROFILE: THE INSPIRATION

The first thing that awed me about The Smacktivist was that they were still in college when they first started playing roller derby. Even as a person overloaded with responsibilities, the idea of being in school full-time *and* working *and* playing roller derby was unfathomable to me.

The next was their incredible skating skill.

Max "The Smacktivist" Schneider
(Credit: Candace Moser Stafford)

Mack had started at OSU as a club ice hockey player, having grown up playing the game. Their transition from blades on ice to wheels on concrete was no issue at all. The muscle memory is the same.

And then later, once I got to know Mack better, I was awed by their incredible ability to set a goal, work hard, and make it happen. Whether it was opening a skate shop in Columbus, captaining the team, or scoring points, Mack's dedication is apparent. And most recently, they demonstrated that dedication by first going to grad school to become a clinical mental health counselor at New York University. Next, after moving to NYC, they tried out for Gotham Roller Derby All-Stars and have since become an integral player on the team. Mack played with Gotham—in their main jammer rotation—in the world championship game in November 2019. That was a goal set during that Ohio versus Gotham game in 2013.

I know we didn't plan it, and I can't even recall if we ever talked about it, but 2015 was kind of a "Year of Yes" for Smacktivist and me. We were both somewhat known in derby at that point—Mack as a breakout player and I as a leader in WFTDA. We were lucky enough to get new opportunities as a result, and we took a lot of them. Both of us ended up doing a lot of things we'd never done in roller derby before, and we ended up doing a lot of it together. We played on the coed pickup Team Berzerker, made up of both WFTDA and Men's Roller Derby Association skaters from teams across the Midwest, and we both traveled to Rollercon, an enormous roller derby convention that takes place annually in the July heat of Las Vegas.

Neither of us are the type to visit Vegas without roller derby, so we kept ourselves busy that week. I taught classes on derby leadership,

Mack played in a worldwide all-star game, and both of us took baby steps into banked-track roller derby for the first time. That week was the first time I think Mack had to reckon with the prospect that they actually might be famous in roller derby. Like everything else in their life, they handled the awkwardness of having peers as fans with their characteristic grace and positivity.

I watched them navigating this new role—derby superstar—with complete humility, and the same kind of agility they demonstrated on the track. I also saw that the public face takes a private toll on anyone who is that visible. We were not social butterflies at Rollercon. We spent quite a bit of time under fluffy comforters in our over-air-conditioned hotel room, decompressing from the sensory overload that the convention can be and avoiding the glaring lights of the Vegas strip almost completely, and for Mack, decompressing from newly realized celebrity.

—Amy Spears

I never got to skate with The Smacktivist, only met them in passing, so I'm going to promise I have no bias here. Mack played with Ohio Roller Derby from 2011 through the end of the 2016 season, which is right when I got my skates back. At the time, Mack ran a skate shop in Columbus and set me up with new lime-green wheels and giant Gumball Toe Stops. They were taking a break, they explained, but would probably be back in 2017 to do some coaching. When I went to a practice and said I met Mack, Birch explained, "Don't you know? Mack was maybe the best player on the entire team. Have you ever seen them skate?"

I had not. During the 2019 championship games, OHRD gathered at one of our local sponsor bars to watch playoffs. We are not a quiet group, so we are put in a back room full of TVs and chicken wings. Whenever Mack took the track, we got real quiet. We watched them dodge blockers with an easy grace, turn one skate slightly right to curve around a pack, then wind back around the track to the very same spot in seconds. Mack's control is breathtaking, their head on a swivel, always seeking the other team's jammer even as they bust through the opposing team's pack. As Mack jams, Mack blocks. Mack is multitasking, Mack is both playing and watching gameplay. Mack is then adjusting movements accordingly, helping teammates and pushing with an incredible strength. Mack's skating is skilled and complex and delicate and brutal, an undeniable art.

—Kegel Scout

A Word from Amy Spears, Washed-Up Roller Derby Skater

I've mentioned the jobs we do to keep our individual leagues running: making the flyers, paying the bills, setting up the track. WFTDA, the organizing body of the sport which I'd been volunteering for since nearly the beginning of my derby career, is run the same way. By the Year We Went to Champs (that is capitalized inside my head every time I think about it), I was one of five officers in the organization, charged with overseeing committee heads of a particular pillar of our business, and reporting to the board of directors. My pillar was membership, and I oversaw everything having to do with member leagues coming into the organization from all over the world: meeting the requirements, training them how to be roller derby leagues in the off-the-track sense, policy writing, creating procedures and enforcing them. We might have had scheduled breaks from gameplay at this point in the evolution of roller derby, but you can't take a break from keeping the main infrastructure association up and running.

I remember next to nothing about the two seasons after the Year We Made It to Champs. We played almost as many games, but with new captains and coaches and missing key players. With Bunz gone, we had holes in both our jamming and blocking rotations, but The Smacktivist began to come into their own and make an even bigger name than they already had in derby.

Our laser focus on the 2013 champs had not let us prioritize developing a breadth of talent for the future, so we kind of had forgotten how to. We struggled to develop other younger players in both 2014 and 2015 and relied heavily on a small subset of vets who were still around. We didn't totally tank, but in contrast to 2013, it often felt like failure.

More than that, my focus had naturally shifted from gameplay to the more administrative side of the sport. In May 2015, I was elected to be vice president of the WFTDA board of directors, and that meant a lot more travel for meetings and a lot more time spent on off-the-track work. At one point I added it up, and between games I played and travel to tournaments and meetings for WFTDA, I spent over a month in hotel rooms for roller derby during 2015. Getting all that done while also making enough practices to maintain game eligibility was becoming an increasingly difficult proposition for me. And I wasn't having the fun I'd had in years past. I was slowly coming to the realization that something had to give, and that maybe I was going to retire at 10 years after all.

Even though so much about our culture had changed, I had still lived those earlier expectations from when we had first started, and the idea that leaving the track was somehow a failure was hard to shake. The guilt that came from needing time off felt crushing. I hadn't taken a break through so many things: buying a house, moving, switching jobs, the deaths of several family members, a broken nose, a breakup. Feeling like I needed a break from derby because of derby was horribly ironic and somehow felt wrong.

Now it's so much easier for me to see that most of these things I pushed through were times I needed a mental break, not necessarily a physical one—though sometimes it took physical ailments to get me the mental rest I needed. This time, I vowed that I would make the right choice for my psyche. I told no one.

Deciding to not skate the 2016 season might have been one of the hardest decisions I've ever made in my life. It already felt like failing somehow. I'd always wanted to leave before I became irrelevant on the track. And now, maybe it was that my self-image had been beaten down after a year of throwing in everything I could physically, followed by two years of never feeling like we could measure up to what had been, rarely feeling like I had worth on the track. Or maybe I truly wasn't at the top of my game anymore. I no longer had the perspective to really know, or the mental capacity to delve into that question too deeply. So whether I liked it or not, something had to give.

I have friends both in and out of roller derby who like to tease me about how I failed at retiring, but a large part of me always intended to come back. I couldn't tell anyone I had that intention, on the off chance I liked the free time so much that I changed my mind and would have to admit that I failed in that regard too. I had to couch it in jokes to avoid feeling like I was letting everyone down. I told people I was on the "ten years on, one year off" plan—as if this were actually a thing that existed. Even though I was giving myself a break, I was still setting myself up with fail-safes. Leaving felt so risky. "We'll see," was my standard answer when someone inquired if I would ever return to skating.

The WFTDA has always prided itself on working from within. Other sports might have commentators and back office administrators who once played the game, but for us, they often do both at the same time. Committee heads face each other on the track on a Saturday and then hold online conference calls the following Monday. Doing both is how it has always been. So, I tried to be clear and upfront. I even posted to the WFTDA that I was taking time off skates specifically to focus on the admin side. I didn't mention that something had to give and that I probably needed a break from all of it. Instead, I kept my board responsibilities and stopped playing the game. I was openly criticized by some, who saw me as "just another nonskating board member"—ignoring that all of our board members had skated for multiple years, whether or not they currently did. Ignoring that not everyone's body could last forever in a contact sport played on roller skates. And definitely ignoring that not everyone can—or should—do it all, all the time, forever.

While some in the derby community questioned how I could do a good job as a board member if I wasn't playing the game any longer, it was an easier sell to my non-derby friends, who saw that I was overloaded but maybe didn't understand the drive. They teased me about how soon I'd be back. To counter the latter, I vowed not to even join up with our recreational league yet.

Regarding the former, I suffered the pain of their comments in silence, feeling like maybe I deserved it. This was, after all, my version of failure—failing at "doing it all."

I'd always prided myself on being able to handle multiple jobs in derby. I could be a trainer at home, and have a committee job, serve on the board of directors of WFTDA, and be a core blocker on our charter team. Multiple years I was the recipient of the Can't Sleep award at the end of our season, given to the player who seems not to sleep because they're getting so much done. And my peers in WFTDA were those same people in their own home leagues.

I didn't feel exceptional because I surrounded myself with other people like me in that way. On one hand, you can read this as proof of the sort of dedication that's exhibited by a select group in this sport. On the other hand, when so many people are going to these lengths, purely of their own accord, this kind of all-encompassing commitment can start to feel like a de facto requirement. There is a pressure to be all in, all the time. And when you view that through the lens of this being a primarily female community, in light of the kinds of pressures our society puts on women to do it all and have it all, it can start to feel a bit like a type of internalized misogyny.

I didn't want to admit it, but I was at my breaking point. Not that I had too much going on necessarily, but I was beginning to find things I wanted to do that (gasp) weren't related to roller derby, and I couldn't figure out how they would fit in to my life. My schedule was a well-oiled machine with absolutely no room to spare between work, WFTDA, OHRD, and a standing once-a-week date to see my non-derby friends, which was only possible because they were willing and able to meet me at 10:00 p.m. on Wednesday nights after I was done scrimmaging. And I was beginning to feel like all the on-track work wasn't worth it. I wasn't having fun playing roller derby that season.

I had always planned to do what Pippi and Bunz did—let everyone know that I'd be retiring before my last season even started. But as things got increasingly hectic, I realized I was going to have to do something on a shorter timeline. And so, after our 2015 playoff, before our team roster had even been chosen for the next season, I wrote a post and put it on our forums.

I referred to it as the "little *h*" rather than the "Big *R*"—it was *hiatus* not *Retirement.*

I left the door open to come back. I said I'd still be around. I offered to coach our B-team, Gang Green. But I also made a promise to myself not to put skates on my feet and not to take on any other official jobs with the league.

Then Chainsaw and Bigg Rigg asked me to help coach the charter team. In a move reminiscent of that first season when I promised myself not to be on the board and then almost immediately agreed to be on the board, I said yes.

I didn't at first. I tried to beg off. I told them I wasn't willing or able to travel to all the games, that for one of the home games I'd be in England on official WFTDA business for the Roller Derby World Summit, and that I wasn't committing to coming to scrimmages every week. They called my bluff and were fine with that. And so, I ended up bench coaching both teams that year. Wearing an *A* Sharpied on my arm with my black-and-green dress to designate me as the coach who could interact with officials for Gang Green and carrying a clipboard to run player lineups for charter.

I did make good on my promise to myself that I wouldn't take on other things, though. I didn't go to practices except at the height of the season. I didn't take on other jobs. For the first time in 10 years, I didn't feel like I had two full-time jobs on top of my full-time job. Instead, it was the one extra, with the WFTDA board.

And though my non-derby friends didn't think I could do it, I actually didn't even put roller skates on my feet for almost an entire year. I wore them at my last official game, the Skatemare Before Christmas in December 2015, then didn't put them back on until I dropped in to rec league scrimmage the following November. The worst part of the intervening months was that my feet hurt so incredibly when I awoke every morning. I couldn't figure it out until Ms. D'fiant, a fellow WFTDA board member who had experienced the same when taking time off for maternity leave, ever-so-cheerfully said to me, "Oh, that's all those tiny muscles in your feet atrophying."

I'd had no real plan for what I would do with my newfound time. I purposefully didn't plan it out, knowing if I did, I wouldn't have time to relax and instead would end up filling it and the year would be over before I knew it. I did decide I wanted to take some classes. Since I work at OSU, one of the benefits is free tuition. So I signed up for a nonprofit management course, to help out with the WFTDA board gig. I took a few weeks of aerial classes, but the studio was a decent drive so I didn't stick it out. I bought a new (to me) car from a former teammate, cut my hair, and adopted my first dog.

I didn't miss skating. I'd thought it would be hard to be on the bench. Hard to advise players when I wasn't in the thick of it and hard to see my friends taking the track without me. I knew I had needed this break when I realized I was fine with this new role and didn't have the FOMO I'd expected.

And then, in June, I had to miss a game coaching because I was in Australia as part of my WFTDA board duties. The Great Southern Slam is the biggest roller derby tournament in the world and takes place in Adelaide every two years. Five tracks simultaneously for three days. Forty teams competing. Constant games. WFTDA sent me as one of our ambassadors to meet with the Australian and New Zealander teams, to listen to those who were members, and advise those who weren't yet. And along the way, we got to watch *a lot* of roller derby. This was the first time I felt the FOMO, watching all these games from teams of every ranking and skill set. Skaters from a half a world away who were living the same life as me, or at least the same life I had lived.

It was that week, in another hemisphere, when I made my decision. I had traveled halfway across the planet with my friend Kim H. Fandango of Derby City (Louisville, Kentucky), and I told her, "I think I might come back to skating." That's as far as I was willing to go out loud. But I'd made the decision.

7 O-H-I-O

When I introduced myself as Kegel Scout to Ohio, they were stoked. When I offered them "Scout" as a less graphic alternative, my teammates—my people—insisted on calling me Kegel, no Scout necessary. I made three rec league practices in August 2016. Tryouts were in September. I hurtled into derby as I had before, this time older, wiser, more lactose intolerant than ever.

This was not the game I had briefly played, had less resemblance to the freewheeling chaos I remembered. It only took the three rec league practices before tryouts to realize if I joined a roller derby team again, it was not going to be on a lark. I would have to invest myself wholly, because Ohio had their shit together. I don't say this in derogatory comparison to any other team in WFTDA. I only mean it was clear in Ohio that folks couldn't get away with half-hearted commitment. They had made a name for themselves with less than half the resources of coastal teams. This team had roots, had been around the block, knew what it was like to be unpaid, near-professional-level athletes. They were relentlessly self-made. It was intimidating.

Tryouts were both on and off skates. The training committee gauged not only our skating abilities, our WFTDA minimum skills, but also our balance, strength, and ability as general athletes. They took note of our squats, planks, burpees, push-ups. I kept up well enough. Of around ten potential skaters, I felt like I was in at least the top three. The training committee also held interviews. One at a time we'd sit before a group of three Ohio veterans to answer questions about our work ethic, athletic tendencies, our exposure to derby. I did not sell myself as a triumphant returned skater, but a ding-dong who broke her back and once, as a ten-year-old, excelled at basketball. Everyone laughed, but not as hard as I did.

Our last exercise was skating laps. To be cleared for game play at the time, a skater had to be able to skate a minimum of 27 laps in five minutes. Whether an issue of endurance or form or mental stress, it can take rookies months to get over their 27/5; many folks have the skate skills and game knowledge, but if they cannot get over that last hump, those damn laps, they can't play. I was the only Fresh Meat to pass the test that day. My breathing failing, my sweat leaking all over the concrete, I tried to demonstrate a quiet humility to my potential teammates. When I finished tryouts, I phoned approximately 11 different people. As each person answered, I'd say, "Guess who was the only person to pass the laps," and before they could answer or tell me I had the wrong number, I'd shriek, "IT WAS ME." I made the team.

Amy Spears came out of retirement one day and did not seem to remember me. I was relieved. I planned on taking Ohio very seriously and hoped I might even fly under the radar as I eased back into workouts and got to know my teammates. I did not want to appear more foolish than I assumed I already did.

I then spent my first year with Ohio as team mascot. My fellow rookie, Sun of a Birch, and I wore a lot of green, though the costuming was random and always in flux. We wore dinosaur onesies several times, in full gear, and skated through the stands demanding crowd participation in a wave. I ordered my dino onesie online, mostly because of the butt flap beneath the spiked tail. I did not anticipate how drenched I'd get cartwheeling on skates, had no idea I'd drip puddles of sweat on the floor as I demanded more wave participation, but this time *make it slow motion.* When we (I) got too tired to throw candy at people, we (I) sat near the merch table and joyously snacked on bite-size candy bars as we cheered on our team.

Another bout, Birch wore an inflatable Slimer costume with a tiny motor inside to inflate it. I dressed as a grandmother that day, mostly because I wanted to wear sweatpants and a gray wig. I'd pretend to be old and less mobile right before I executed several toe-stop cartwheels. Near halftime, I had Birch-turned-Slimer drag my derby granny character across the floor. I can't remember why, but I was building a narrative for the crowd, and they were responsive. I streaked a snail trail of sweat over the concrete, left a granny body outline where we stopped. In her efforts, Birch busted the Slimer motor. The green ghost hung off her like baggy, synthetic moss. I hoped the team was realizing our potential. I wondered if perhaps I was better suited to be a mascot anyway.

Birch started rostering on the B-team and I was happy for my derby spouse. I was sad for me but knew I was not yet ready to get body-checked in front of a crowd. Hesitancy is dangerous in full-contact sports. When you hesitate, you make mistakes. Hesitancy undermines precision. The only thing I felt precise about was choosing the right mascot wig. It was new and strange, being thoughtful about my body's needs.

I would not play my first game until the very end of that first season, in a C-team level game, composed of our not-yet-rostered league skaters. I barely registered my MFA graduation in spring 2017—everything seems less important when the president is a full-blown fascist—and felt more excited than I had in years on the drive to get my ass beat in Akron. My first bout with Ohio Roller Derby was unsanctioned, essentially a uniformed practice with strangers. LGBTease drove us in their Subaru Outback. The air-conditioning was broken so I began sweating as soon as we hit the highway. Hardkore fed me baby carrots and told me to focus my nerves into my squat. Stay low, low, low, low, low, low, low, low, I thought.

When we arrived at the Akron convention center, I ran to the toilets and did not soil my green plaid spandex. It was a miracle. The Akron team was large and mean. Elektra coached us, her long, blonde ponytail commanding calm, like Elsa in *Frozen* but colder. Halftime, I almost barfed. Second half, we got our asses kicked. I think I had a really good time. Then we drove back home. I was mindful in the game, emphasizing process over product, trying to reframe my ideas about winning and losing. Moderation isn't easy when one is used to doing everything or nothing.

In my second year, I was elected to the OHRD board of directors as the head of bout production. I needed to prove I was in it for the long haul, that I had something to offer even as I built my skate skills. As I finally had enough control over my body to roster with Gang Green, our B-team, I was also the lead for all bout-related issues. I was a panicked puppet and Elektra pulled the strings. At her orders, I became a de facto event planner. I oversaw venue needs, outreach to visiting teams, fan engagement, halftime events, score projection, announcers, MVP awards, and organizing people to set up the track and bleachers. I still acted as mascot for charter team games, then mopped up my first round of sweat, changed the bandanna under my helmet, and prepared to play with Gang Green. My involvement with derby was daily, sometimes hourly, online sending production or marketing emails. I attended monthly board meetings, helped with our introductory derby classes at the rinks, and slung beer at festivals to earn stipends and tips for the league, all of which culminated in a more than part-time job. The pay was invaluable: I was hanging out with my first-ever sports heroes as I learned what it meant to be an athlete.

When I started training harder, and looking for inspiration, Chainsaw lent me *Sports Psychology for Dummies*. I searched for other sports books featuring, or at least written by, women, and instead I found a March 2018 article in *Esquire*. "The 30 Best Sports Books Ever Written" does not include a woman. None of the books listed are about or written by women. Not a single one.

My general attitude as a child was "Put me in, coach!" I had a winning smile and a thirst for outside validation. I had, have, all kinds of those cheerful traits many girls develop so they might have a say in their own world. I volunteered first. I left last. I did many things, most of which were not specifically for me but benefited others. That does not mean I did not benefit from things. I did. I always did well on tests because I asked a lot of questions, once I realized the best teachers wanted to teach. The bad teachers were mostly . . . well, men, particularly the football coaches and basketball coaches and wrestling coaches moonlighting as social studies teachers. Those teachers left me alone if I left them alone, and if they thought I was funny, I could duck out during their lackluster "history classes" to haunt the English department, where the teachers (mostly women) appreciated my involvement and curiosity. As early as second grade I knew to temper my know-it-all nature with a dash of forced humility. My hand was up, and I would knowingly comment about my hand, way up in the air again. I let people know I was in on the joke. I wonder, from here and now: Did I portray myself, my motivations, as a joke?

Where else might I have channeled all that energy? How could I have ever known, growing up, that I was athletic? That I could thrive in a sport? That my skill in processing quickly and critically might be applied to movement and game play strategy? Based on what I saw on TV, at school, I understood *girls'* sports, and later, women's, as a series of footnotes in the history of sports overall. There were sports, and then there were *women's* sports. Little wonder I recognized it all as something I'd never need to take seriously or as something I understood as irrelevant to my life. Why bother when people spent their time skipping that part of the story?

I remember my mom saying once that my little brother, Ronnie, was always on the move. He couldn't sit still, couldn't stay in one place. He needed to be kept active. Busy. He was Bart Simpson, incarnate. But I remember suffering the same kind of energy. I read through it, buzzed from book to book, played neighborhood-wide hide 'n' seek, did mine and sometimes other people's homework, and killed at street kickball games when I was finished practicing my alto saxophone. My sister, Daisy, and I spent hours cleaning the shed-turned-clubhouse in our backyard, and when we finished, we'd drag our torn trampoline up to the clubhouse porch. Then we'd spend an hour or more jumping off the roof to the trampoline, hollering as if the 5-foot drop were 20. The older I got, the less available physical activity seemed to me, a girl. I take credit in some of it, as I usually didn't want to put in the necessary effort. In middle school I joined and/or was allowed onto the girls' basketball team, Go *Lady* Trojans, but I never trained hard enough to be a point guard or starter or of much use to the team as a whole. My own laziness landed me as power forward or center, not to imply those positions take less effort. The lazy descriptor is all mine, me. I was just enough taller than the rest of the team at that point in my life. Those extra inches were all I had to offer. We all knew I'd been stationed below the basket as someone's last ditch effort. It became clear that what I did best on the court was—*SPOILER ALERT*—peacefully absorb a full-body hit. But the truth was more complex: when I didn't take my body, myself, seriously, because I didn't know how to, didn't understand how my body fit in with the world presented to me, my reframed "laziness" also gave me an out. If I was not good at basketball, it was because I chose not to dedicate myself to it fully. If I didn't win, it was because I wasn't invested in winning to begin with. If I lost, I lost on my own terms.

In high school I'd heard swimming was the best exercise for burning calories. My friends agreed to try out, too, which led to my being the worst swimmer on my high school swim team. Go *Lady* Trojans. To further supplement my attempts at a Britney bod, I stopped eating soggy cafeteria french fries.[1] Sometimes I also stopped eating lunch, after I'd skipped breakfast. At my first swim meet, I came in dead last among the slowest-ranked freestyle swimmers. Still competitive, still fighting with underdog gusto, I swam so hard I got my first, and what I assumed would be my last, sports-related injury: I popped my left shoulder out of, then back into, socket. I sobbed post-race, but when I tried to blame it on the pain (a solid 9 on a scale from 1 to 10), my mom believed I was just embarrassed for losing. This wouldn't have been out of my character. I also knew X-rays and MRIs would cost more than the worth of my mom's beater van. So, I walked it off. Instead of enduring the pain at practice, I splashed around the deep end. I started belly flopping with my sister on the dive team, or flipped off the boys who left basketball practice early to creep on us in our swimsuits.

I find roller derby players to be an anxious, thoughtful, thinking people. The ass bruises may suggest otherwise, but the game is incredibly cerebral. Many of my teammates are late-in-life athletes, and I imagine they, too, have always been busy little bees. They are Renaissance women, all. Kloverkill, with purple mullet, split tongue, tattoos, body piercings, can craft an amazing Krampus costume out of any material. Her day job is as a surgical tech, and her other job is cracking my shit up (Klover: so funny, so ferocious). Pain Train writes and draws and pursues social justice even as she earns a master's and works full-time. Betty was serving in the Air Force when she joined a league in South Korea, and these days she juggles school,

---

1   I did not.

jobs, single mom status, and, as Avocado Toestop says, "ruining lives on the track." Burnadeath is a social worker, a former gymnast, one of my favorite people ever, who founded her own roller derby league in Oregon in 2006.

I don't have questions about why it took me until my 30s to have a warehouse full of sports heroes. We all know why it took so long, even as the women, transwomen, transmen, and nonbinary athletes I've met are talented, hard-working, inspirational, kind, generous, brilliant people. What I want to know is how long will it take for this to change? How long will it be until women's sports are televised as often as men's? Who still needs convincing that watching women play sports is as thrilling—or more so—than watching men's?

I think the American in many of us gets stuck in underdog narratives, or obsessed with winning instead of journeying, because we're afraid of irrelevancy. We're afraid of being average, just like everyone else. But the answer to adequacy is not rendering everyone else a loser. We aren't all constantly winning *or* losing, because we are so much more *process* than *product,* ad infinitum. This binaried win/lose scenario also reinforces simplifications of sex and gender, which has direct effect on the best sport in the world.

In less grad school speak, why can't all sports played by all people be respected and valid? And why can't all people be valid and valued? Why must we decide *if I am not A, then I am B,* when it may be easier to accept there isn't just A or B? Complexity in the world is the most common thing of all. There's a whole alphabet, a spectrum of letters. If we continue to reduce our understanding of life to win or lose, man or woman, masculine or feminine, important or not, we hinder all of us, however we identify.

I have always been loud, motivated, less than feminine. When sports didn't come easy, it was almost a relief. I'd already struggled knowing fully who I was with minimal backlash—how could I even consider male-dominated athleticism? Instead, I focused on study. I played music. I daydreamed on the trampoline. I learned how unlikely it was to be a gymnast like Kerri Strug or Dominique Dawes, so I didn't bother to try. I still practiced poses, mimed floor routines on the playground, but I figured that was as good as it would ever get.

That sucks. And I am so grateful to know better now, to have unlearned. But.

How much longer will I have to insist on the realness of roller derby? And how much of that insisting is in response to the boundaries our culture builds between gender and sports?

To be present in roller derby is to be past, present, future. I'm talking mindful, controlled anxiety, if such a thing is possible. There are so many things to keep track of in live play. Where is my jammer? Where is their jammer? Was that whistle for me? Should I head to the penalty box?

Where the fuck did Kelsey Khaos just come from? Ope, here is, no, there goes Trix. Stay low, Kegel. Bend your knees, Kegel. Squeeze your abs, Kegel. Trust your blocking pack, Kegel. Roller derby is full-bodied thinking.

On practice days, two to four times a week, I only think about practice. From the time I open my eyes to the moment I'm fully geared, I'm thinking:

I *GET* TO SKATE TONIGHT.

Notice the word *GET* in italics. There are variations on a theme, here. *Get* is on a good day. Occasional days, *Get* complicates and turns into *I have to* or *I need to*. When I'm not on my period, it's often *I want to.* On particularly difficult days the phrasing is altogether more like *I'm too old for this shit.*

My enthusiasm about attending practice depends on any number of factors. Am I hydrated? How hydrated am I? How hellmouth hot will the practice warehouse be, how bitterly cold? Am I prepared for the cold sweat? Am I too tired? Did I eat too many black beans for late lunch? Was late lunch more like early dinner? Am I going to get body-checked by Bruss Knuckles, then hurl all over the track? Am I going to shit my pants? What if I have to go in the warehouse, in the port-o-potty? What if I jam and this jostles something loose in my stomach?

Does my back/knee/shoulder hurt today?

There are also nights, post-practice, when I get home at 10:00 p.m., 10:30 when there are car accidents or snow—and I stumble to the shower and think, *What the fuck am I doing?* My lower back throbs. Not all the time, but enough. I'm in my late 30s and when it's cold it feels as though my knee might burst, so I cross-train and stretch and use that stupid awful foam roller.[2] I am covered in fingerprint bruises. People make wife-beating jokes, and the joke's on them; domestic violence is never funny. Also, watch out, I'm the one serving beatings.

Four years into roller derby, and I have an eclectic list of accomplishments. I fouled out of two Gang Green games at a tournament in Milwaukee, after which I bawled in the locker room. Most people rarely experience a sad Kegel, and my teammates looked a bit panicked, unsure how to approach me as I sat in a corner, stared deep into a locker and sobbed. I let it all out, then I changed my clothes and recorded statistics for the charter team. I am usually the emcee for our biannual derby galas, though Shayna Scully and Sheepskate are coming in hot for my performance-related league jobs. I love my body most days. I love my abiding ass every day.

I have lived, so long, with a case of Despite. I think Despite even applied to being a girl, and then a woman. I wanted to be competitive and assertive, Despite being a girl, and when I got pushback for my ambition, I spent much of my life trying to be at least *physically* smaller. Now I am an athlete in a sport where my size is the prize. I have heard many people say that roller derby is about taking up space, and I'm doing that now. I am not trying to lessen, and I will not apologize for being more. I'm busy being. I have never been so in tune with my own body. I think I've discovered I'm proud of myself.

Yes. Proud. This is a confusing feeling. There's like a rolling, green breeze in my ear and I don't need to cry but I wouldn't mind if it happened. I'm not concussed; maybe this is what contentment with oneself is like. Imagine my surprise, that it was here in the America of America all along, my pride. I am proud of my earned aches and pains. I am proud of my strength and courage. I think Ronnie would be proud too.

I'm always happy once I get to practice, even as it's so damn hard to get there. As we tie up our skates, strap down our protective gear, Vyles and I riff potential names for women's body-shaping garments. We agree *Chunx* is the best one. We practice stops until my thighs give out. I drink two full Nalgene bottles of water, and a small Gatorade. I sweat-hug volunteers and skating officials, like Gnome, post-scrimmage, to their dismay. We end the evening all hands in. We chant *Ohio Roller Derby,* so we don't forget who we are.

---

2   No I don't.

Zee "Loraine Acid" Aria
(Credit: Candace Moser Stafford)

OHIO PLAYER PROFILE: THE FORCE

The first time Zee showed up at an OHRD event was at a "wannabe clinic"; it was sometime in our second year, a skating night at a local rink where those interested in joining could meet current players in a low-stakes environment. I didn't have a conversation with her, just overheard bits and pieces, but I will never forget how she looked on the track.

She had long, dark hair, curly and tousled, spilling over her shoulders. She wore a tie-dye shirt, tight cutoff jean shorts, rollerblades, and wrist guards. She could clearly skate already, but her style was unorthodox. She was even doing crossovers on the turns. Inexplicably, she was somehow doing them with the wrong leg crossing, yet still ending up with the proper trajectory. She didn't try out for Ohio Roller Derby and become Loraine Acid until 2009, after the demise of home teams. She laid low at first, feeling shy of fitting in with the group as a whole, mostly hanging out with the friends she brought along with her to volunteer as officials. She quickly became a staple of Gang Green, as her unorthodox style made her incredibly hard to block, her lower half never quite going where her upper half seemed to predict.

It was when she made the charter team that she began to shine and click with her friendships in the league. She "derby wed" Ava Tarr on a bus trip to Nebraska, walking down the aisle of the charter bus, as our coach BFF sang Europe's "The Final Countdown" in a falsetto. (I have never again heard the familiar "do-do-DOO-do. Doo-doo-DOO-doot-do" without remembering this moment.) She started using her real name on the track—a major decision for her, given that she'd long gone by Zee. Her actual name, Turkish in origin, was difficult for some people to pronounce. She was even mulling over the need to change her last name to something simpler for professional reasons when she became a dentist. We still called her Acid.

She became known regionally and beyond as a jammer, a blocker, a pivot, and effective at all three. Her opponents respected her not just for her tenacity on the track but also for her cheerful demeanor at the after-party. She often sought out people at the bar who she knew she might have made big hits on during the game to make sure they were okay, that everyone was still friends. Somehow, Acid stuck with OHRD not just through her undergraduate career, but also through the entire time she was in dental school. The latter time period also saw her making custom mouthguards for her teammates. It was during my hiatus year that Acid started making these, and when I returned, she was adamant about getting me one. Our busy schedules made it difficult for us to meet up, which is how we ended up with her doing dental impressions on me in a hotel room outside Detroit after we played a game there, before we woke up to play Ann Arbor the following morning.

Somewhere, there is a photo of her holding the dental tray in my mouth as I sit in one of those chairs that is always crammed into the corner of a hotel room for no clear reason. Two players brand new to our team look on, as if this is the most natural and normal thing to bear witness to. Balancing professional school and roller derby was a big challenge for Acid in terms of time management—as it would be for anyone—but her commitment was never in question. She once flew to a tournament in Wisconsin even though she could only make it for our last game of the weekend because she had to take her dental board exams on Friday and Saturday. Because of how our first games went, we ended up playing at 10:00 a.m. on Sunday, so she basically came from the airport directly to the venue and geared up just in time for the first whistle.

Eventually, she graduated with her dental degree and decided to move to New York City to do a dental anesthesiology residency. After just a few games in 2018, she left OHRD, then landed with Suburbia Roller Derby and played with them while working on the next part of her career.

Her reputation both in Columbus and beyond came from both her eternal smile and her exceptional ability to channel her compact body into a leveling force.

And from her tendency to be late to everything. Absolutely everything.

—Amy Spears

A Word from Amy Spears, Derby Lifer

Late in 2019, in a whirlwind trip to Pittsburgh, I played my 175th WFTDA-sanctioned game. We think that's a record. There's no easy way of knowing, because it's not like it was a priority to set up this sort of recordkeeping when we first got going. I'm reasonably certain that if it's not a record, no one has played all that many more, just based on the fact that Ohio has played more games than any other team and that the number of players who have played since those early days is dwindling. I won't call us a dying breed, because a surprising number are still here—playing, officiating, coaching, announcing, super-fanning. We're not dead yet. I planned to hit 200 sanctioned games in 2020, which is a nice round number, pleasing the part of my brain that thrives on organization and fun facts. But I wasn't going to go out of my way to push it. When it happens (if it happens), it happens. It's season by season now.

I run into former teammates from those early days every once in a while. Sometimes they drop into a game and express that this is a different sport from what we played those early days. They say they are not nearly so badass as to be able to play what has evolved. I think they are wrong, because clearly they were badass enough to jump into the complete unknown so early on. They ask how on earth I am still here, still skating, and I beg off a little. I blame the luck of having had no truly major injuries while playing, that the business side of things is running along swimmingly, in part due to their early efforts, and that after one term as WFTDA VP, I declined a nomination to run for reelection, so I have all this glorious free time now.

Ha. Ha ha. No I don't. It's just more reasonable now.

I've seen many people leave roller derby, and Ohio Roller Derby, during my tenure.

Many have gone because they found something new to focus on, wanted to start families, move somewhere else, go back to school, focus on career. Some have just said, "Well, I did that, and now I'm done." And a small subset have rage-quit, hitting a breaking point and then taking their toys and going home. When I ask myself why I haven't done any of those things over the years, the only thing I can point to is that I've been willing to change. I've evolved with the game. Whether it's because of the stage of life I was in when I first came in or whether I'm just good at change, I don't know. But at some point, if you're going to stick it out in a community like roller derby, where everyone is running the show in some way, you're going to have to give up the control of something. Or everything.

I saw a meme recently and the general gist was if you want to be happy as you get older, you should not shake your fist at whoever the millennials or Gen Z-ers are when you are boomer age or yap about how it wasn't this way in your day. You should realize that it is no longer "your day" and that the world and structures in which we live have evolved, and that what you would have done back then is not as relevant. The people actually living a particular experience probably have a pretty good read on it already. This feels true of roller derby, and probably sped up tenfold. The sport is under 20 years old and has already endured multiple critical eras of growth. We're not in a vacuum. We exist in the larger changing world, whether we like it or not. I have teammates right now who are literally half my age. Their mothers are my contemporaries in many cases. Buffalo Saucy's mom played for Queen City in Buffalo, New York, and when she told me this, we did the math and realized I've probably played against her mother. My co-captain, Kelsey Khaos, cheerfully told me once that she had been at our very first game, and the things she remembered were HellionBOI, Pippi RipYourStockings, and being afraid of the lobby escalator—because she was 9 at the time. (I was 29.) I do not understand half of the puns in the derby names my younger teammates choose, and they look at me blankly when I explain that no, I did not read Harry Potter as a child, because it did not yet exist. It's weird for me, and it's weird for them. But they're the ones molding this now. So I will regale them with tales of the old days and will condense episodes that consumed my life for weeks or months into fun little pithy anecdotes. I periodically punctuate a sentence by uttering #derbygrandma, which I am sure they love. There's nothing like someone 20 years your senior actually pronouncing the word *hashtag*. I will remember how we built the sport, the community, when I first joined Ohio Roller Derby, and I will respect how we're all still building it.

I don't know how long I'll skate. I don't want to not skate, which at this point is just as good a reason as any. Derby fits in my life and doesn't wholly consume it anymore. After I hang up the skates, I'll probably still stick around. I've already dabbled in officiating a few times over the past year, and I like to make myself useful.

Kelly green was my favorite color before OHRD, and it probably will still be after. I've put down firm roots in Columbus, so it's unlikely I'll ever transfer and play for another team. And while my heart will always belong to WFTDA, ultimately, it's Ohio that made me, and broke me, and let me make myself again. The 2020 season was to mark Ohio Roller Derby's 15th on the track, and it would have also been my 15th, with an asterisk about how I didn't skate that one year and took a break, but kinda didn't, because I was still traveling with the team to coach and also serving on the board, yada yada yada. The aches and pains that plagued me through my early years of roller derby have mostly ebbed. My knees feel okay. I have picked up a cross-training hobby in aerial—like circus tricks aerial, trapeze and silks and such. I am still covered in bruises, just from multiple sources now. Plus, my body is such that I'd be bruised if I were sitting on the couch, so no big deal.

As I write this, in my 40s, I feel better than I have in my life.

The 2020 season was shaping up to be pretty spectacular. At the end of every year, everyone in OHRD fills out an Intention Form, indicating if we plan to come back the following year, if we want to switch up roles and move from skater to official or a volunteer role. As the human resources coordinator, it's my job to track everyone down and get the form filled out. So I was excited at the end of 2019, when every single person on our charter team indicated they were returning to skate. In all the years of our existence, that was unheard of. We'd had years when a large crop of people was returning, but having no retirements at all was kind of a big deal. A couple people were nursing some small injuries, but for the most part, we were all healthy. We'd had a good season that steadily built momentum and success, and we were getting back to that point where not only did our individual players have experience in the sport, but they had experience playing together. That's where you want to be.

On top of that, we had just taken in the largest rookie class we'd had in years. LGBTease once joked that it wouldn't be the beginning of a season if we didn't have the largest rookie class ever—a joke that was funny because it was largely true. Our recreational league had been feeding our rookie classes for a few years, and this time, not only did we have a dozen rookies ready to take the track, but they were positively *driven*. I've never seen a rookie class so dedicated to skating outside practice and asking vets for off-skates workout ideas. They were setting themselves up to be a force to be reckoned with, and their energy was good for the entire organization.

With the whole charter returning, basically an entire team roster's worth of rookies and a vast majority of the very solid crew of Gang Green skaters returning, we had grown to nearly 50 active skaters—the largest the league had been since the month of our very first game in 2006. While still much smaller than a lot of other leagues, we'd grown so large that we had to reorganize the way we ran our weekly scrimmages to prevent having 20 people sitting on the bench getting cold (and believe me, in a warehouse with no climate control in February in Ohio, we're talking frigid), so we rented additional space in our warehouse to make multiple activities at the same time possible.

And then, January 6, 2020, we got a shock. I will never forget the way that afternoon unfolded.

It was an unusually sunny and mild Monday for January in Columbus. I had been in a new job at OSU for about three months, just long enough that I was getting the hang of things, but still feeling things out and learning the ropes. I was in the office, checking in on our OHRD training committee forum online just after lunch. Another trainer, Kelsey Khaos, had just shared a news article with the rest of us, simply saying, "I think Acid is mentioned in this."

I clicked the article, expecting to see some sort of accolades about her dental career or maybe a mention of her recent inclusion on the statewide New York roller derby team going to an upcoming pickup tournament. I was fully unprepared for what I found.

The article was about a bus crash on an icy Pennsylvania highway that had happened over the prior weekend. I was confused, thinking Kelsey had maybe pasted the wrong link. But as my eyes skimmed down the page, I hit Zee's name. The way the newspaper had printed her full legal name meant there was a little confusion in our minds—was it her? She'd changed her last name to make it shorter and more pronounceable recently, and they used her full first name that not everyone even knew, so the weirdness was jarring. But her name was unique—the idea of someone else having the same one seemed statistically improbable at best.

The bus had been on its way to Columbus from NYC when it hit the ice on the mountainous highway in Pennsylvania and careened off the road. The article mentioned just a few injuries despite accompanying photos that looked horrific. It only named two of the injured, and one was Zee. She'd been ejected from the bus.

I was already thinking about how we could determine what hospital she was in or if she was maybe out already, wondering if she'd gotten to Columbus or had gone back to New York. I was flipping back and forth from our chat conversation and the article. Just as my new boss walked up to ask me a question, I clicked the link again. My eyes skimmed back to that sentence mentioning Zee.

The article had been updated in those few seconds since I first read it. I didn't understand what I was reading. I couldn't find the mention of Zee where I had seen it just seconds before, and when I did see it, I held my breath. My brain was going too fast at this point and I wasn't reading things in order. I needed to slow down. I apologized to my boss and asked him to hang on for a second because I needed to read this.

All of this happened in a split second, but it felt like hours. I can remember every little bit of it, like I was following stage directions in a play. And then there it was in front of me.

The sentence in the article no longer said Zee had been injured in the crash. It now confirmed she had been killed. My poor boss, who of course had no idea what I'd just read, got treated to a rather stream-of-consciousness spurt of word salad, as my brain went into coping-with-a-crisis mode.

The six of us on the training committee had to sort through our confusion. Some of us had clicked before the article was updated, some after. All those things that people go through during grief were now hitting all of us as we text chatted. Most of us were at work. Elektra wasn't online or in the conversation at all at the moment, and we wanted to make sure one of us talked to her before she read this confusing chat. I suddenly remembered Ava, a recently retired skater and Zee's derby wife, who was a professor at OSU. I knew she was back in the country after a semester-long sabbatical but didn't know if she was physically on campus. The trainers continued to talk about whether to let the league know or wait until we knew Zee's family had been informed. I think we were also still hoping there was a mistake, that there would be a retraction and we wouldn't have to have these conversations at all. Nevertheless, I started walking across campus to see if Ava was by chance in her office. I dreaded having to be the person who told her, but I didn't want her to be alone reading this news either. She wasn't there, and I was walking back to my office in the now obscene-seeming January sunshine when my phone rang.

It was Kegel. I answered the phone and heard her say, without pause, "Amy, is it true?" I didn't have to ask what she meant. I sat down on a bench behind OSU's library. I inhaled, and just said, "Yes."

The second they found out Zee had played roller derby, reporters had a hook for their articles, and they started contacting both Suburbia Roller Derby and OHRD via social media and email to get our raw reactions. The New York media started contacting us first, and soon Columbus outlets joined in. The careful plan the training committee had begun making to ensure this was public knowledge before breaking the news to the league, to carefully inform our friends—Zee's friends—was over before it started. A couple of the people assigned to monitor the email accounts that received press messages were new enough to OHRD that they hadn't even met Zee. It was rattling.

It suddenly dawned on me how many former members we had now living in other cities who I didn't want to find out from social media or by seeing a news report. I emailed Deadeye, who now lived in California and had been very close with Zee. I sent a Facebook message to Ena Flash, who was in Calgary. Kitty Liquorbottom called me, having heard already, and we went down a list of retired members we needed to tell. She would call Bunz, in Seattle, and Pippi, and BFF, and some others closer to home. It was during that conversation I suddenly thought of The Smacktivist, who was in grad school in New York City. I wrote and rewrote a message to them about 70 times. By the time they got it, they had heard already, and we shared our anger and our hurt in an Instagram chat. Mack had just seen Zee in person in New York that week.

I got back to my desk. My Facebook inbox had multiple messages from reporters. Chainsaw had finished up a message to post on the forums to the league, having had to now amend it to include information about how to handle the press.

I knew I needed to have a job, to keep myself busy to avoid just emotionally imploding and shutting down, so I offered to field the press inquiries. It had been my job in the past for the league—albeit generally with a far more promotional and cheerful bent than this. I talked to one of our photographers about allowing the media to use action shots of Zee. I declined on-camera TV news interviews. I was candid with a reporter I'd talked to before from the *Columbus Dispatch* about the way it felt having to deal with a barrage of press when we had all found out 20 minutes earlier. I told him that several people were just informed by reporters, looking for reactions to the news, that their close friend had passed away. He expressed empathy for this. It was not included in the article.

I did not share with him my simmering rage that despite the fact we had to fight tooth and nail to get the press to cover our sport in terms of gameplay and on-track accomplishment, they wanted to display our shock and raw grief to the world. That, despite the fact that Zee was a top-level roller derby player, an amazingly ambitious person, full of joy and enthusiasm, they hadn't clamored to talk about her life until it was over.

The next few days were a blur of social media messages and reconnecting with old teammates. Zee's family planned her memorial service at a nature preserve an hour or so away from Columbus. It feels odd to say that it was the best funeral I've been to, but it was by far the only one I've ever attended that felt helpful for my grief. It was muddy, it poured rain the entire time, and we stood in an open, brushy field. There were so many people there, the saddest roller derby reunion ever. Most of us didn't know Zee's family, and hearing them talk about her, mentioning the same things about her that we would miss—her joyousness, her generosity, her collections of odd objects, her perpetual tardiness—was overwhelming and bittersweet. I took the long car ride with some of the old guard derby folks. Three of us were probably the only people who knew about every roller derby person who attended, which made it all the more surreal. We sobbed in the cold rain and the mud, hugged each other, and said goodbye. I finally cried. I had teared up of course, but at the funeral, I finally let myself sob, hugging Bigg Rigg awkwardly as we both wielded umbrellas, having just seen our friend lowered into the earth.

Because our season was approaching, we already had a couple of league social events planned, and one had already been scheduled for the day after Zee's memorial, January 11. It felt awkward to have something happy on the calendar but even weirder to cancel, because what were we to do if not hang out together? Plus, we had this giant rookie class who had largely never met Zee in person, who only knew her as Acid, who were already navigating the strangeness of being amidst a giant new group of people who had suddenly plunged into deep mourning. They may not have known her, they may not have known a lot of us for long, but they were still supportive and wonderful.

I'll admit I did almost bail on attending. I'm glad I didn't, because while I couldn't have known, it would be one of the last official social events we'd have for well over two years. In the end, what won out was that I wanted to be around people who knew Zee, to be around my friends, old and new. So we had that chili cookoff, and I went.

As usual at our social events, it eventually evolved into feats of strength, as people bench pressed and dead lifted each other, Nick Tater and Bigg Rigg attempted the lift from Dirty Dancing, and a large group of us built a human pyramid. A few weeks later, Zee's mother, far away in Turkey, saw our photos on social media and thanked us for remembering her daughter this way. Peach Roulette pointed out that the base of our pyramid was made up of a mix of brand-new rookies and the longest-term vets, completely by coincidence. It was fitting, given it would be the last photo of an Ohio Roller Derby event for a very long time.

8 Derby Veteran

In 2020, I was entering my fifth year with OHRD, nearing six years in the sport—a sport where players average a three-year derby career. As 2019 stopped and 2020 started, I intuited, in my IBS-riddled gut, 2020 was the year all my piece parts—my arthritic back, the depth of my squat, the scream in my knees, the anxiety in my head and shoulders and belly, and my long road to thorough comprehension of the sport itself—all would come together, call a truce, and propel me forward like the competent rolling banshee I'd always dreamed I'd be.

Competence is highly underrated.

In January, we finished a draft of this book. Amy Spears, Derby Icon, and I had done a thing that felt more impossible than a toss of Bigg Rigg over the apex: we had finished a draft of a book. A sports memoir, no less! Amy and I were content with an ending that was all hope and love and derby bliss.

I started training for 2020 in December 2019. I'd decided if I was trying to be an athlete, then I already was one. This season I would focus on trying rather than winning. At the beginning of our 2019 season, team captain Amy Spears awarded me a swinger position—not as in sex party participant but as in the potential to play for both teams (still sounds like a sex party, I suppose). I'd be a starting player for the B-team but also a developing player for the charter team. This meant double the practice load if I fully committed to my potential, my trying, and I was committed to committing: I would move into the 2020 season officially a near-official member of the big kids' team. I had aspirations. Manageable ones.

I remember most of January and February of 2020 like an "Eye of the Tiger" montage, sub the Rocky soundtrack for Lizzo's "Tempo" because I'm not a boomer *and* I have a dump-truck ass. I trained most days, slow and steady, repetitive in the best possible way. This would be the part of the movie where Kegel wipes her brow with an Ohio Roller Derby wrist sweatband, which can be purchased here: www.OhioRollerDerby.com.

I've always wanted to star in my own sports-informed movie montage. For the first few months of the year, I willingly participated in strength training classes with my teammates, wherein we flung around 50- or 60-pound bags of water or sand. My dad did this shit for a living when I was a kid, hauled roadside bags of things to and fro. Here I was, paying to use a fancy camouflage leather bag of water with straps when I could have instead gotten paid for hard labor. Turns out any latent athleticism I have is only blue-collar baggage. I excelled at lifting and carrying. We lunged with water bags. Squatted with water bags. Overhead pressed with water bags. Carried around water bags. Water bags are like sandbags but unruly, disagreeable and sloshy, the water in constant movement, our bodies having to fight against it.

In between practice days and voluntary bag lifting, I added in yoga and intense, near-violent stretching. I biked as the days got a bit warmer, chased the minimal hills of Columbus. I wore my soft gray OHIO ROLLER DERBY sweatshirt like a safe, comfy good luck charm. At work, teaching English as an adjunct instructor at a community college, I occasionally veered into proselytization of the greatest sport in the world, but the students didn't seem to mind. This was another job without health insurance, but Obamacare came in clutch and allowed me to keep skating and hitting and falling and squealing. At the beginning of 2020, I felt strong and ready to hit or be hit (this, I did not disclose to my students). I wore my skates in my basement. I strapped my helmet on to protect from the low-beam open ceiling, my knee pads to guard against the slant of cement. I watched game play on YouTube. I cleaned my skates.[1] All I wanted was to eat, sleep, and play roller derby.

January 6, 2020, I got an email from a local reporter asking about a former player of Ohio Roller Derby. She used Acid's legal name and I did not recognize it. It's strange, but I would likely not recognize most of my closest friends' legal names. If someone at practice yelled Sam instead of Kegel, I'd have an identity crisis. Our names are a part of our community. They are special and exclusive and only given to those who are most committed to leaning on one another. We are, in name and identity and sport, collectivist. We are not, cannot be, ruggedly individual if we want to play together, and we love, love, love to play. It's how we find joy. I mean, also some fear (hence the leaning on each other, literally, mentally, metaphorically). To be a solid roller derby team, we have to be very in tune with each other while also with ourselves. If that sounds too woo-woo or not a masculine enough sports metaphor, I guess I could say . . . we're like a Rube Goldberg machine, only functional together, in disrepair apart.

Turns out masculine sports metaphors aren't my thing.

We each do our part, but as one. We are mindful of each other because we are mindful of ourselves because we are mindful of each other. I'm saying there is no *I* in this shit.[2] We are our best selves when we collectively take care of each other. I think this is what some people call being a team.

It was unfathomable that a friend, a teacher, a goofball, a teammate of ours could be dead. *A bus accident on the Pennsylvania Turnpike* . . . the reporter had to be wrong. I did some interneting, read that the bus had been on its way from New York City to Columbus. The reporter was right. Acid was gone.

Acid was my first trainer in rec league practices. Enthusiastic and patient and in love with skating, Acid was remarkable when teaching.

---

1   I really did.

2   Though, as our copyeditor pointed out, there are literally two *i*'s in "this shit." Thank you, Tyler, whose derby name is now The Strangling Modifier.

She was silly and weird, and so fucking talented. I remember entering a practice early one night and Acid was already on the track, in an old cropped OHRD jersey and jean shorts, on wheels for as much time as she possibly could be.

Acid loved to lead practice. She was great at breaking movement down, describing the side of her body she leaned into, the way her feet and legs and hips worked in tandem and landed in a squat plow stop. Acid was quite literal, so she would have described it like, "Well, first I tilt my butt and hip back in this way but then, like, squeeze my thighs—hold your core in, too—yeah, then swish your skate like this, like *swish*."

The restraint she had over her body was astounding. It was a poem, the way she danced away from blockers, then glided into other blockers, her shoulder checks always landing and debilitating. The depth of her bend was unmatched as she hauled around the corners of the diamond, her black braid a rope whipping behind her. She'd jump three feet off the ground at full speed and soar over the apex. She taped her fingers together so they would not break because she was in school for dentistry and she planned to play hard every single time. Acid took big risks, was a happy thrill seeker. She embodied joyful play.

Acid moved through the world like every situation was a jam. She juked in grocery aisles, practiced footwork in the dental school, her feet crisscrossing as she moved from one mouth to the next. She'd street skate and bounce off cracked sidewalks and crumbling concrete stairs, moving so fast she was gone before you'd even fully realized she'd been there all along. I spent my first year with OHRD watching Acid more closely than any other player. She jammed less and less because she had been concussed far too many times, but she blocked and pivoted as only an intuitive once-jammer could. She was a Jack-of-All-Trades and also a Master-of-All-Said-Trades. Acid rolled so low to the ground that when she moved up into an opponent, she brought all the power of the floor with her. Any time I took a hit from Acid, I saw stars, then her ceaseless grin. After, she'd always offer a loud apology.

"Sorry, Kegel!" she'd shout, already flying through the opposite side of the track.

When my practice backpack finally broke under the pressure of stinky, heavy gear, water bottles, and extra wheels, Acid offered me a rolling suitcase. It was zebra print on the outside, hot pink on the inside, a very Acid bag indeed. She had purchased it for her dentistry supplies but it was too cumbersome, she decided.

"Are you sure?" I asked.

"Yeah Kegel, c'mon. You can buy me a beer sometime."

Acid spoke to everyone like they had long been her friend. I thanked her, fangirled and thanked her, and Acid gave her cheerful smile and said, "Yeah, Kegel! Put it to good use."

Cheerful. Acid was cheerful and hopeful and excellent and kind. A very, truly, good person. And now Acid was gone. The team was wrecked. Chainsaw cried, and that is as shocking as, say, a global pandemic. Several memorials were planned. The news kept mentioning some kind of flu going around, the presidential election was also making everyone sick, and Acid was gone.

What kind of year *was* 2020 going to be?

On March 7, just 12 days from our March 21 opening bout of the season, I went to what would be my last OHRD practice for the foreseeable future. This wasn't exactly foreseeable then—a *then* immediately *before* full-blown COVID, before loss of time, end of community—but perhaps it was premonitory, my sudden burst of nostalgia for my home away from home, even as I stood present in its dusty bowels. I filmed a panoramic shot on my phone, our shitty warehouse practice space dark but for bars of streaming sunshine through the industrial windows.

It was a Saturday practice and there were few of us. Most folks prefer to attend the weekday evening practices, but I've always enjoyed an occasional Saturday morning practice. It's peaceful at 10:00 a.m., and somehow there's less practice pressure because it's technically a day off, and sometimes we brunch after Saturday practice.

No brunch that day. People were on edge and wondering if things were about to get shut down because of the coronavirus. That was the rumor, that we were all going into quarantine. Here is when the smart, early believers had already begun stocking up and running the most necessary errands. That day I was the last in the building. I flipped the switches off and the fluorescent overhead lights flickered, died. The warehouse is different silent, no whistles or cackles or skates skidding, no construction machines drilling and banging on the barely walled-off north end of the building, just eerie silence and shafts of dust-orb filtered natural light. Cleaning this place is always a bitch, but when sunlight beams through the windows of the cavernous space, the dismal morphs into calm, even peace. The sun was so sweet I filmed a wide shot of our home in the dark. I posted it to the 'gram and wrote, *I love our gnarly home. I love my team. #OhioRollerDerby.*

This would be a memento for a memorable season, I knew it. I was going to finally roster and play full-time for charter. I was going to live and play extra hard, for Acid. I grabbed my zebra and hot pink print gear bag, rolled it past our sinister rented porta-potty, and locked the warehouse door behind me.

COVID-19 never had to play out like this. The incompetence of a large body of mostly White men in power put us here. I am furious at their incompetence, their ego-driven ideas, their relentless selfishness. My point might be a controversial one, but I stand behind it: if the Women's Flat Track Derby Association ran this country, life might still look a lot more like 2019.

Here we were, in the midst of a horrific and preventable global pandemic. A totally preventable and unnecessary global pandemic fumbled by a garbage US government and maintained by said government's uncritical or bigoted fanbase. Our country, too terrible to come together as a team and wear masks and get vaccinations and do what we can to play together, to regain community, to help one another, to live.

Have these people ever even heard of a Rube Goldberg machine?

When the world shut down mid-March, I was prepared to miss our opening bout. I truly expected we would still have our remaining games. We would head to Ontario for the Put Up Your Toques Tournament. We would sojourn to Rochester, New York, and to Philly, and host Madison. We would play a home bout in jean shorts, in honor of Acid. We would have a ceremony to publicly retire her number, 59.

We would, we would, we would.

From where I am now, it's wild to think back to March 2020, that my most immediate concern was game time. Finally figuring out hockey stops. Not fouling out of a game in Canada. That was a different life. Things escalated quickly. Now we live in a world that will always be pre- or post-COVID-19. People continue to die. The pundits continue to lie. Rhyming isn't what it used to be, and without my team, everything was, has been, so much harder, so much bleaker.

By the time we hit April 2020, OHRD knew the entire season was bunk. The OHRD board of directors scrambled to cancel games and keep us all aware of the ever-shifting policies and updates from the international governing body of the sport, the Women's Flat Track Derby Association.

WFTDA reacted faster and more thoroughly than any other sports organization[3] in the world. On March 13, 2020, they released a statement announcing a COVID-19 Task Force, online open forums for community discussion, and the necessity of following local protocols as we collectively navigated the virus and its impact:

> As a sport that takes inclusion and safety seriously, community spread is an issue we must prioritize. COVID-19 concerns aren't simply about contracting the virus ourselves, but also protecting our most vulnerable community members. Anything less than that is ableism that threatens the lives of others.
>
> —WFTDA COVID-19 STATEMENT

March 13 was also the day the president declared a national emergency, even as he had spent the whole of February comparing COVID-19 to the flu, telling reporters that "heat, generally speaking, kills this kind of virus" and then reiterating different versions of the same statement. February 23: "We have it very much under control in this country." February 24: "The Coronavirus is very much under control in the USA." February 25: "About the coronavirus, which is very much under control in this country." February 27: "It's going to disappear. One day it's like a miracle, it will disappear." February 29: "Everything is really under control."

---

3 And several governments . . .

On March 16, Trump announced new social distancing guidelines, after consulting professionals, the likes of which included his son, Trump Junior: "I've spoken actually with my son. He says, 'How bad is this?' It's bad. It's bad. But we're going to—we're going to be, hopefully, a best case, not a worse case. And that's what we're working for."

That very same day, WFTDA posted the following to their website:

Dear Membership and Community:

During the past 48 hours, the WFTDA Board of Directors and Staff hosted several meetings along with the COVID-19 Task Force and Competitive Play Task Force. The meetings focused on addressing short and long term planning in light of the COVID-19 pandemic.

We are also continuing to work with our National Governing Body (NGB) partners, JRDA, and MRDA, to collaborate as much as possible on public responses.

At this time of year, our member organizations are playing games across 23 countries to contribute to their competitive season and rankings. Our members are understandably concerned about the impact of health restrictions and travel bans.

Here's what we are doing:

The WFTDA Competitive Play Task Force and WFTDA Staff are working on immediate steps and contingency plans to attempt to preserve the regular season and postseason schedule as much as is possible and responsible.

The WFTDA will host a meeting for Recognized Tournaments in the coming days, in order to work together to make prudent decisions as a community for those events.

The WFTDA Board of Directors, Staff, and Task Forces will be meeting once a week to review new information about the pandemic and discuss how it will affect our 2020 competitive structure.

Recommendations to WFTDA Membership as of March 16, 2020:

The Board of Directors is advising member leagues to suspend training and competition at this time.

Follow the advice of your local public health officials and NGBs when deciding to resume activities.

As WFTDA moved forward with shutting down roller derby, they consulted professionals like Bubble Wrath, BG Smack, and Trauma, US-based derby players who also moonlight as a biostatistician, an infection control nurse, and an epidemiologist, respectively. As derby dimmed and moved further and further away into the future, the NBA used their monies for a Disney bubble and resumed game play with virtual fans. The NFL changed little to nothing, depending on the team. As roller derby leagues across the country began to give up practice spaces and bout day spaces due to insufficient funds, men's professional football and basketball and hockey and baseball and soccer never fully stopped. They canceled games, they sometimes canceled fan attendance, but whatever their COVID protocols, they were never in a position where the fate of their team's entire future hung in the balance.

Roller derby teams are nonprofit and community based, though often not exactly community supported. In Columbus, where the sports industry has long boomed, you'd think we'd have the kind of financial security that would keep a league of our stature and legacy running for decades to come. You'd think we'd own our own warehouse, our own game day space. After 15 years in a city, as a founding member of the WFTDA, you'd think our existence as Ohio Roller Derby would be a given.

It is not.

And because we only function, only *exist*, if we sustain each other, we kept paying member dues so we could keep paying rent on an asbestos-riddled warehouse so we could live another day without actual game play. We were having "practice" via Zoom. We were driving derby parades past each other's houses on birthdays because drive-bys were the closest we could get to hugs. As Frida Killo said in a Zoom board meeting, we would stay apart for each other's safety and hope the game returns while "everyone else is just out there licking toilets."

OHIO PLAYER PROFILE: THE FOREVER ROOKIES

There are 12 Ohio Roller Derby skaters who have not yet played roller derby for the team. They are the dozen skaters that made up that last giant rookie class who joined before the pandemic began. They were motivated, on skates and off. They worked their butts off at practice, and plunged headfirst into their jobs for the league in social media, in finance, in marketing.

They showed up to the orientation I ran before their first practice—with notebooks. No one had ever showed up with a notebook before. They asked questions, and wrote in said notebooks. And I will love them forever for that, among other things.

One of the things that happens after orientation when you come into the league is the assignment of a big sibling. This is a veteran skater who is there to help guide a rookie should they not want to ask questions in front of the whole group or if they need to be pointed toward the right person to ask. Toward the end of 2019, after the rookies came in, someone came up with an idea of drawing out the "family trees" of big and little siblings, and we held an Awkward Family Photo contest.[4] If it wasn't already apparent that this crop of rookies understood us at a very deep level, it would have been from the zest with which they threw themselves into these awkward families. They proudly wore denim, donned animal onesies, went full goth, posed with a food truck, without question.

They just *fit.*

So it was particularly heartbreaking to see them navigate this pandemic roller derby hiatus. They dubbed themselves the FOREVER ROOKIES because by now they should have had little siblings of their own. They should have had two seasons of roller derby under their belts. The fact that they have stuck it out is a testament to how much they want this. They ran for elected positions in the league and are helping to organize our return. And they probably skated more than anyone during our pandemic time off. I was a little scared they'd surpass me immediately once we got back to practices, to be honest. But that's okay, because every few years a roller derby league has to reinvent itself if it wants to survive. And right now, surviving is what leagues are doing, so I'm thankful they are here to be our reinventors.

—Amy Spears

---

4   Amy and Kegel are in the same family. Perhaps it goes without saying, but our family won the Awkward Family Photo contest.

A Word from Amy Spears: The Season That Never Happened

The opening game of our 15th season was set for March 21, 2020, against Steel City Roller Derby of Pittsburgh. The first time we'd played them was in 2007, only our second interleague game at home, and over the years we'd played them more than most of our other opponents. They were relatively close geographically, and in rankings most years. They started the same year as us, so we'd grown up together in some ways. The makeup of their team was similar to ours: vets who'd been there the whole time, transfers from other places, new talent who'd climbed the ranks. And like us, they were climbing in rankings again, so it was a great matchup.

I was captaining the charter team again for the 2020 season. I decided I had one more year in me to do that. With a team of returning players, it was largely administrative, and motivating a team who'd worked together so much was easy in the great scheme of things. As usual, I'd done a lot of rankings math, and I thought we could set a reasonable goal of getting into the postseason tournament with an advantageous seeding, coming into a tournament in the fall with a seed of 5 or 6 rather than 10 or 11 as in recent years. WFTDA had made major structure changes to tournaments since we'd gone to champs in 2013, so that kind of seeding didn't mean a potential world champs run this time. But I wasn't up for that kind of all-in mentality anymore anyway.

The charter team planned to honor Acid by wearing jean shorts for this first game. She had showed up to her first pre-tryout event skating in jorts, and continued to wear them for games and practices for years after, so it seemed a fitting tribute. The board voted to retire her jersey number, 59, at halftime.

It wasn't just OHRD's 15th season and my 15th season—it was also WFTDA's 15th anniversary, so it was to be a celebratory year throughout the sport. The international championship tournament was scheduled for November, in Austin, Texas, where the creation of the Texas Rollergirls had ended up being the creation of our entire sport and where the first official champs had been held in 2007. It had been a few years since I had been to a champs tournament, and I missed the regularity with which I would see my friends in the larger derby community since leaving the WFTDA board of directors. So while I hadn't bought my plane tickets yet, I was planning on being there. It would be a homecoming and a big family reunion all rolled into one.

In February, some of our skaters played for Team Ohio at the Battle of the All-Stars, a pickup tournament of all-state teams that happens annually in Pennsylvania. Acid had been on the roster for Team New York, and they posted that weekend with the hashtag #59forever, her name remaining on the roster rather than replacing her with another skater. Little did we know this would end up being the last major roller derby event of the year worldwide and the only time any OHRD skaters would actually play in 2020. Or 2021.

The first weekend of March, we had Jilleanne Rookard from Detroit Roller Derby come to Columbus for a weekend-long clinic. An Olympic speed skater, she's one of the top jammers in our sport. We invited her to tweak our technique, shore up our derby skills, and prep for our season. After seeing how our rookie class performed during that clinic, I had high hopes not only for our charter team and Gang Green but also for the futures of our newest skaters.

When planning out our season, we had decided to go to the East Coast Derby Extravaganza in Philly for the first time since 2009. I was incredibly excited about this, since I was the only skater on our charter team who had ever played at that event, which featured three tracks running games simultaneously and a swimming pool right outside the venue.

There was so much to be excited about, but there was something bigger going on in the world. It didn't feel real yet, but we'd been hearing news stories about a virus that had shut down several cities in China, and then Europe and beyond. It seemed inevitable that it would come to affect us in the US, but it also seemed impossible because we couldn't see it yet. I'd had a student worker return from winter break from his home in China who had called off sick preemptively one day with cold symptoms to be safe, but other than that, no one seemed worried about this.

The first hints that there would be an effect on roller derby started when communication from tournament organizers began to shift from determining good game matchups and which team would wear which jersey color to talking about what would happen if an event had to be postponed. It seems entirely strange from my vantage point today to think about the incremental way in which it feels like we handled the COVID-19 pandemic initially. As lockdowns and quarantines began, individual games were called off. We had a game involving a Canadian team traveling to us that was optimistically postponed rather than canceled.[5]

On March 12, the governor of Ohio announced a ban on events with more than 100 people in attendance, which effectively canceled our home opener, scheduled for March 21. We went to work trying to find out when we could reschedule with the state fairgrounds and if Steel City wanted to come on another date. Clearly, we had no idea what was coming.

Looking back at the emails now, it's clear we thought that this was a sucky way to start our season but that we'd be back on the track in a month or so. And then by the end of the month, when East Coast Derby Extravaganza and all of our other tournaments were completely canceled, we still figured it would be autumn at the worst and that obviously we'd have to majorly reconfigure our season as a result. By early May, it was pretty clear our regular season wouldn't be happening, but a few people were holding out hope that the low-stakes off-season games we usually played privately in the fall and winter could be reconfigured as our regular season for 2020. But that would also never end up happening.

Now it seems a bit silly that we had even the smallest shred of hope that the 2020 season would happen—or even that the 2021 or 2022 seasons would happen. At this point, I'm somewhat hopeful I'll get to play roller derby before I am eligible for an AARP card, but I'm not sure I'm even holding my breath for that.

We went from two- or two-and-one-half-hour practices on Mondays, Wednesdays, Thursdays, and Saturdays to . . . nothing. Games taking up 75 percent of our weekends between March and June to . . . nothing. Even the meetings dwindled. Team meetings weren't needed because there was nothing for the team to do. Nothing for the captains to plan. Training committee had some planning meetings but it became a time for us to stare at each other's faces through computer screens, trying to remember what our friends looked like. I imagine board meetings were much the same, with the added stress of seeing the financials. No money coming in for almost three full years now because there's been

---

5   But then again, our ramp-up to our return has been just as incremental. We have remained cautious, since Columbus's COVID cases have continued to be the worst in the state, even as the pandemic nears its third birthday.

no derby to play, no tickets to sell. Just a paltry stream of dues payments from our skaters, who by and large have stuck it out.

You might be saying at this point, "But wait? Other professional and amateur sports went back to playing. They may have had cardboard cutouts for fans or sequestered themselves in intentional bubbles, but even contact sports are being played. What's up with roller derby?" It's true. When it didn't feel like things were coming back as quickly as the rest of society, some backlash did arise among members of our own community. As every other sport on the planet went back to business as (almost) normal, it could feel like we were the only sport still waiting. There were leagues who lost venues, either because skating rinks failed as businesses due to the fact that no one wanted to be exerting themselves indoors recreationally or because they had no income to cover exorbitant rents charged for empty warehouses. Some skaters found hobbies (including street and park skating) to fill that time otherwise monopolized by roller derby, and so they retired before ever coming back.

One of the greatest advantages of the wide-ranging backgrounds of roller derby players is that when we are faced with any challenge, we're able to find people who play the sport that have relevant experience. So when it first became clear that COVID-19 was a global concern, WFTDA put out the call for those people. They were able to create a task force of players, officials, and others involved with or in close proximity to roller derby who were physicians, epidemiologists, people with degrees in public health. And they put together a plan to guide leagues on how and when to come back. The plan had seven tiers, from noncontact roller skating in small groups, stepping up through contact, larger groups, playing your local teammates, playing close by teams, and finally culminating in what we had become accustomed to: international competition with fans in attendance. The plan was dubbed "Lives before Laces" to help make clear the fact that while roller derby may be a critical component to so many of our lives, it isn't worth risking anyone's health or life to get back to it in the middle of a global pandemic.

Put another way, we weren't being so selfish as to pretend that skating around a track crashing into each other was important enough to risk even one person getting sick—or worse.

The plan is thorough and has become a model for some other sports organizations. It was even featured on *Full Frontal with Samantha Bee* a few months prior to the US presidential election, the correspondent musing, "I was just wondering if you could take over the whole country?" It's good, but it's one plan in a world full of less-thorough plans or those that were more quickly abandoned when conservatives shouted to "reopen the economy" in spite of the danger we all still face.

At the same time, the feelings of every skater were, of course, different. Some wanted to be back yesterday, risk be damned. Some complained that roller derby was sacrificing so much more than the public at large. That wasn't untrue, but others countered by asking why we shouldn't still stay off-skates if it was the right thing in the larger sense, if all those others were flouting risk.

Because roller derby is nothing if not different from other sports and from the world at large. We pride ourselves on this, so why should this be any different?

By mid-summer 2021, the case rate in Columbus plateaued. Things were looking good enough that we started to plan more earnestly for an actual return. Then the Delta variant hit, and up the rate went again. Schools had gone back in session in person at just around the time we first thought we might be able to return to practice and have a reasonable shot at progressing.

And then the breakthrough cases began as vaccinated individuals began to test positive. Anti-vaxxers and our flimsy-spined state governor, Mike DeWine, had all but mandated we would stay in a non-contact, skating-with-nine-of-your-friends limbo for the foreseeable future. But just as we thought we were going to have to take the idea of going back off the table, WFTDA revised the plan yet again, deeming it a *recommendation* rather than a *requirement,* recognizing that in some countries, things could be almost "normal" again, even if much of the US was still risking infection with everything we did. Now we no longer had to track local case rates, doing our own math to determine two-week rolling stats as politicians had stopped releasing the numbers we needed to promote the narrative of everything being "just fine." Now we had one simple metric—the vaccination rate. Once that was at 40 percent in our local area, we could get back on skates in small pods of skaters. And at this point, in late 2021, we were amazingly already there.

And so, it once again became a question of personal comfort level. Did you feel okay about skating in a dingy warehouse with no running water, knowing that if you should get hurt, a trip to the ER might mean the opportunity to sit in a waiting room of COVID-positive people for hours before getting attention?

Finally, we started to creep our way back toward normalcy. At right around the time we would have normally been going on our winter break, to give ourselves time off for holidays and avoid icy evenings in the warehouse, we were going to be taking the track. We divided those skaters who were ready to risk a return into three separate pods, and assigned each a night of the week to avoid mingling. We went back wearing masks, and at first, we didn't do any contact drills. Training for a contact sport with no touching is a challenge, but we blocked traffic cones, shadowboxed with padded columns, and struggled to balance yoga balls behind us, moving them across the warehouse walls like pretend opponents.

Part of what gave us some comfort level was that a survey showed that the rate of vaccination among our league members was 100 percent—many of us having gotten our shots at the drive-through vaccination facility set up by the Columbus Department of Health, able to see the venue we play games in while we waited in line to check in. Teams across the country had seen their practice and game venues turned into COVID testing and vaccination facilities, so we weren't alone in having pangs of nostalgia while we finally saw the hope of getting out of the pandemic.

Slowly, carefully, we merged those three pods into two, then became whole again and returned to practices three nights a week. On June 30, 2022, we had a scrimmage. We modified the structure to compensate for our lost cardio fitness, but we were actually playing our sport again. There were whistles, accidental sweat smears on concrete, and the now-nostalgic aroma of sweaty gear. We remembered all those things the pandemic stole from us: the sting of Sharpie as your coach writes your number on your Velcro-burned skin, the bump of the rope under your skate wheels as you roll out of bounds.

It had been 847 days since I had last played actual roller derby. Even if it was still just us playing among ourselves, even if it felt so strange and foreign, we were back. It's not the same, it won't be the same, but we're back.

9 We Got Tired

By the time the pandemic hit, roller derby had become the most stable thing in my life. I joined OHRD in 2016, graduated from Ohio State in 2017, and separated from my husband Jesse in 2018. These events fell into one another like inevitable dominoes; my life, once always in geographic flux, found stability through community, and this gave me the time and space to admit Jesse and I were no longer compatible. Joining the team and going to grad school did not end my marriage, but it did change me as a person. My interests and his no longer converged, and though it was heartbreaking, world-shattering even, we realized our relationship had naturally run its course. Through our 14 years, Jesse and I had grown up together. We held each other through great loss and made each other laugh through the heaviest grief. Our 2019 divorce was as sweet and near painless as our marriage had been. We left the courthouse holding hands.

It was early in our love that Jesse said, "I think you might be bisexual, Sam." I'm embarrassed to admit this had not occurred to me before he said it. It made sense. Though I had always considered myself the staunchest of allies, and was never in short supply of gay-boy besties, women loving women—or women loving anyone outside of heteronormative standards—was not a thing I'd been exposed to. In my very limited experience, lesbians or bisexual women were like unicorns: having excellent hair styles, being sparkly and mythical. I did not see them in real life, or in media, or in pop culture, and so, since I was a late bloomer already, a deviation in my sexuality quite literally had not crossed my mind. Like the cultural messaging I'd received about girls in sports, women loving anyone other than cis straight men was far-fetched and happening to people I didn't know, would never meet. It also seemed irrelevant to our life together. Jesse and I were already married then. What did it matter if I was kinda gay?

A lot of people in roller derby are kinda gay. The best sport in the world, its modern iteration, is fundamentally queer: the complexity of the game alongside the camp, the athletic prowess and glittering performance, is as queer as the sexuality of many who participate in the sport. My life was newly surrounded by open queer love through roller derby, and seeing this, I realized I felt attraction to *people,* not a person's gender. Gender was not a hinderance or bonus for me in terms of whom I was attracted to. I was astonished, felt affirmed by the casual affection I saw between same-sex and queer couples. Access, representation, is a shocking, self-revelatory thing—I needed to see myself in the world to fully appreciate and acknowledge my queer self, a self my ex-husband had recognized and loved long before I did.

The first time I tried roller derby, I wasn't ready to be fully realized. I was young, I was devastated, and I was lost. I was compulsively hetero, had only pictured my life with a man, and though I never fully complied with traditional ideas of womanhood or wifedom, I could not imagine an alternative. Then I met a wonderful man when we were very young, and fell in love. I assumed I already knew everything I needed to know to live a happy, full, self-actualizing life. I did roller derby like it was drag,[1] a costume, played as if I could abandon my real self and try something else on for a while. This is also how it felt to be straight—like I was in drag, wearing an itchy, floral-patterned dress, and a choker of fake pearls, attire that didn't quite fit.[2] It took me over 30 years to acknowledge and explore this aspect of my identity. It's not fun coming out to family, especially after having been in a decade-and-a-half-long hetero relationship, and I struggled with what

---

1 A Word from Amy Spears: And indeed, there is so much crossover with derby and drag, especially when it comes to the names. Imagine my surprise, though, when Instagram recommended I follow a drag queen named Amy Spears (no relation).

2 Today I would pair this outfit with some black Doc Martens boots, #gay.

to call myself. In terms of labels, most accurately I might be considered pansexual: attracted to a person regardless of their gender. I mentioned the word to my mom and immediately made jokes about frying pans, Teflon, cast iron, then privately berated myself for making a mockery of myself. I've tried out bisexual, but that still feels adherent to the male/female binary, and my love happens on a spectrum. I've finally settled on queer, the same word homophobes threw around all throughout my middle school days. It sounds right when I say it out loud. I'm queer.

The second time I did roller derby, I was no longer doing derby drag. Instead, through roller derby, I was finally becoming my truest self. I found a community where I didn't have to pretend, where I could be as complex and queer, all strong and soft at once, as I had been all along. I've had to pretend for so long, around cis straight men in particular. I've spent much of my life toning myself down. Sometimes it's easier to just be agreeable. I knew this as early as elementary school. I stopped winning math relays in fifth grade because I saw how it made the boys scowl. I quit begging them to let me play four square because all the other girls had already given up, and the girls were treated better as a result. Most, if not all, women have experienced this: a need to compromise, to downplay ideas and valid anger and valuable perspective, in order to not offend, offput, or even enrage a man. But in roller derby, cis men are the exception, not the rule. I am not a separatist; I am not someone who wants a world without men. I expect as much of men as I do—and have seen accomplished by—women. But it is *so freeing* to be at the center of a culture, to simply *be* without fear or trepidation. Roller derby has afforded me this gift, this freedom, of self.

Kegel Scout is not an alter ego, it's who I am: tough and sensitive, loud and thoughtful, a theater kid and a jock, a queer unicorn. I misspoke when I said that grad school and roller derby changed me as a person. I was not changed; I was revealed.

In the months, then years, after March 2020, I've moved less and less. It is 2023 and my body creaks and cracks now because of pressure and impact and age. My right ankle feels both loose and stuck; a wiggle of my big toe makes it feel like my whole foot is about to fall apart. I churn my foot in circles, clockwise, then counter, and wait as if the snapping and popping will stop if I move exactly right. My back is more arthritic than ever because I've lost the strength my core needed to hold everything together. It is near impossible to muster the energy to skate in the library parking lot near my house because I know the morning after will be Bad. Bending at the waist Bad. Hip socket crunching Bad. I started writing this book in my mid-30s, but 40 is coming in hot Bad.

My post-pandemic body is falling apart Bad.

Even worse—none of that seems to matter all that much most days. The pandemic isn't post yet. There is no normal to return to. I miss skating so hard, so fast that my eyes water, I miss catching jammers with my butt, I miss feeling powerful in all those derby-centric ways—all things that, for me, necessitate having a team. I miss my friends.

I feel defeated.

I'm so damn tired.

Amy Spears, Derby Statistician and general optimist, once told me (and wrote in this book) we have played more games than any other roller derby team in WFTDA—202 was the number. Around the time we hit 200 games, Chainsaw realized she had skated in approximately 75 percent of the total jams our charter team had that year. That would have totaled 460 jams and, as Chainsaw explained, was "the most jams any charter skater in the North America East Cup (and probably WFTDA) skated that season." Perhaps most importantly, this was Chainsaw's first season post–spine surgery, a 360-degree spinal fusion, wherein they entered her back and front to fuse and cut and solder to make her the robot she is today. When asked why, or how, Chainsaw explains: "I don't get tired."

There's a song by the rapper Kevin Gates called "I Don't Get Tired," and I'm going to guess that Bigg Rigg turned the team onto it. The chorus goes "I got six jobs, I don't get tired." To sustain a roller derby team, one must have six jobs. A very slight exaggeration; every single league member tends to have very many jobs. Tired? Who has time to be tired when we've got bouts to put up? The phrase so thoroughly encapsulates the attitude of our league that it's become kind of a league mantra, a very Ohio kind of motto. Back when we used to have frequent karaoke parties, the night wouldn't end without someone taking a mic and yelling "I DON'T GET TIRED." There have been lulls in practice, a tired kind of loud quiet that arises after a series of intense drills, a sonic manifestation of physical plateau. The sweat streaming from our brows, our knees furious, we think we can't go any further, but then someone says, "I don't get tired," and we have no choice but to keep going.

We made shirts. The phrase is so iconic at this point that a few years ago, we designed and ordered T-shirts to be sold at bouts and online. We were fully aware that no one else would understand the #IDGT stamped across the chest, that no one might buy said shirts, that the shirts need a lot of contextualizing to make any sense, and we were absolutely okay with the fact that even if the phrase is an inside joke, at least *we* would have T-shirts reminding us we don't get tired.

But Pandemic Kegel is tired. Pandemic Kegel refers to herself in the third person because she's dissociating. Pandemic Kegel is dissociating, defeated, and angry. Kegel's mom says that anger is actually hurt, and she is probably right, though please don't tell her. Ohio Roller Derby is, more than any other place I've been, my community. My people. I've lived in Columbus for eight years now, the longest I've lived anywhere as an adult. I have roots here because I joined and have helped sustain a community. Our community has a lot of people who've seen some shit. We have a Dead Parents Club support group, and meetings happen as we're walking, slap happy, to our cars after practice. We help each other cope by making jokes about each other having dead parents. There are no other people I'd rather be awkward about death with, no others I'd rather cheer on, no others I'd rather not get tired with.

In 2020, I needed my team for an endless list of reasons. In the years since, we've struggled to come back together in any regular way. We are a deeply selfish nation. Why can't America get its shit together? Why can't we be a community for each other? I've needed my community at a time we could not safely be a community because other people in this country prefer to put themselves before each other.

I miss my friends. I miss dunking on Donald Fucking Trump and then halting a body with my hip. I miss the group of people we are together, how much we learn from each other. I miss laughing with them. I'm a working piece part of a queer Rube Goldberg machine, poorly functioning without the other pieces and parts. It's not true that we don't get tired, we absolutely do, but everything in this world is more manageable when collective. Survival calls for synergy. We do not work if we are a dysfunctional *We*.

I make Ohio Roller Derby sound like a cult, but it's a team. Or a family.

OHIO PLAYER PROFILE: KEGEL'S WIFE

Amanda "Sun of a Birch" Birch
(Credit: Candace Moser Stafford)

The relationships we create in roller derby can be complex, fast, fleeting—an exacting description of the game itself. People don't last in derby. The cost, in time and money and mental space, is great. The cost of medical bills, the ongoing physical damage and re-damage, is greater. Being an adult on a team, especially for those of us who haven't been a teammate since fifth-grade basketball, is intense. It is easier to face insecurity and fear with someone who's going through it simultaneously, and so derby culture's answer to this need is the derby spouse or partner.

Sun of a Birch is my roller derby wife. They are number one on their jersey, and number one in my heart.

Birch and I met at a rookie practice in 2016 it might have even been league tryouts. I remember her in the sit-up position beside me, her little blonde head bobbing. My first thought was "I'm not gonna let this bitch out sit-up me." My second thought was "This bitch is about to out sit-up me." Then they didn't even do push-ups on their knees, which forced me to do several regular push-ups. Like, really, Birch? A person who *already* has well-developed physical strength in their shoulders and biceps?

Who did she think she was, Bigg Rigg?

Later, I found out Birch and I were both in our early 30s and lived down the street from each other. We could commute to the warehouse and worry that 30 was too old for this sport, together. We could practice roller skating on the cracked tennis courts of our neighborhood, and jog at six in the morning. Or seven. Or eight. Or tomorrow.

Birch had only started roller skating that year, and this eased my athletic insecurities, which is sad, because it meant I could only feel good about myself if someone was worse off than I was. This is the opposite of the kind of person Birch is. If Birch were a rock, they'd be tungsten, the strongest and most supportive rock, but gold plated 'cuz it's pretty, and with a bunch of multicolored gemstones because Birch is a Ren Faire kind of hippy and they'd eat that shit up.

Birch is a visual artist, too, an art therapist. Their day job is helping people through what is often the worst time in their lives. She embodies empathy. She listens. Google "active listener" and her face will appear, friendly and inviting. We have these adorable mailboxes with our names and photos at the warehouse, and when they are full of loving, thoughtful notes, Birch put them there. She probably wrote the majority. My first plant came from Birch, and it's still alive—in fact, it's thriving.

It did not take long for Birch, who played softball and volleyball and team sports and did all kinds of physical crap, to far outpace me in derby skills. But by then, Birch taught me we could be competitive, together. We could push one another. We could cry on each other and get drunk after a very difficult bout together. (Birch only needs to smell my bourbon, and they're trashed.) Our rookie year was decently sized, around 10 of us at the beginning, down to 5 or so at the end. Six years later, and it's only us 2. For this, I am so grateful.

—Kegel Scout

A Word from Amy Spears: Democracy and Protest

I have been lucky enough to get to travel—a lot—as a result of roller derby. Playing the number of games we do means a lot of trips, and I also had to do a fair amount of travel for annual meetings and board meetings and tournaments as a WFTDA board member. Often this means I can say I have physically been to a city, but I have not actually been anywhere else. Instead, I am intimately familiar with convention centers, Shriner's halls, and armories across America and beyond.

There is one city I have traveled to more than any other in my derby career, and it's not one many would likely expect, but with regular tournaments and events, I came to find myself there annually, if not more often. To the point where I have actually had time over the course of multiple trips to visit the market by the river, to see some public art works, and finally, after four trips, get myself to a brewery.

That city is Milwaukee.

My first trip to Milwaukee was arguably one of the most important trips of my roller derby career, which I would have no idea of at the time. It was 2008, and the Brewcity Bruisers were hosting BrewCon, that year's annual meeting of the WFTDA.

I should probably back up and explain some things about the WFTDA and about the governance of roller derby in general. You see, as every single task necessary to the running of our local league is completed by a skater, official, or other volunteer, the same is true of the WFTDA. Many of the same people who founded leagues ended up banding together to found the United Leagues Coalition in 2005, which later became the WFTDA.

And something else that's different about roller derby from any other sport on the planet: it's not that the players are in control at every level and that there are no owners or promoters calling the shots—it's that decisions are made collectively. Roller derby is a democracy.

Our leagues elect their leadership. Some have their entire membership vote on every decision; some (like OHRD) elect a board to handle the business. But whether they are direct or representational, they are democratic nonetheless. Any league joining WFTDA is basically required to operate in this way. The early motto was "By the Skaters, for the Skaters," which, after the critical roles of officials, nonskating members, and other volunteers became much more obvious, was amended to "By Derby, For Derby."

Every WFTDA member league has representatives who ferry information to and from their leagues, and who vote on WFTDA issues and elections on behalf of their teammates. All those elected board members and committee heads for WFTDA—they are also members of leagues. Some are skaters playing at the top level of the sport; some skated a season or two before moving on to other roles; some are referees or nonskating officials, announcers, production volunteers.

But all are helping to run what they are participating in and represent the do-it-yourself ethos that roller derby has always had.

But back to Milwaukee.

When the 2008 invitation to attend the annual meeting went out, OHRD only had one WFTDA representative, Ziggy StarBUST. So the board asked if anyone else would be interested in accompanying her to the meeting so we could cover concurrent sessions. Of course, I volunteered. Ziggy, being a school teacher, wasn't able to get away on that Friday, so I'd be there Thursday night and for Friday meetings on my own before she joined me. To save funds, we contacted Grand Raggidy Rollergirls from Grand Rapids, Michigan, who we'd played a couple times by then, and asked if they'd like to split a hotel room. It would be Jackie Daniels, Terrorhawk, Ziggy, and me in a room in a conference hotel near the Milwaukee airport.

I was super excited, but very nervous. Some people would probably be surprised to hear me say I'm an introvert, because I'm fairly comfortable speaking in front of groups and talking shop.

But the thing that makes me seriously nervous is actually the small talk, the one-on-one social situations. So Ziggy and Jackie—whom I already knew—would be the extroverts who would shepherd me through pool time and chitchat before meetings and recognizing people without helmets on—which is a surprisingly difficult skill. And Terror would quickly befriend me, and take me with her in befriending everyone else.

What I was about to learn was what a WFTDA annual meeting actually is. For the past few years, owing to our international growth, travel concerns, and, oh yeah, a global pandemic, they've been held virtually, but for the first decade, they were in person, a Friday, Saturday, and Sunday of sessions to talk about the state of roller derby and WFTDA business and to share knowledge about how best to run our leagues. In the evening, there were social events: drag shows, pub crawls, occasionally a live roller derby game from the host league or mash-ups of the attendees. And the highlight for most of us, a scrimmage with all the people there. Everyone wore black or white shirts and got in a line of 50 or 60 skaters, and then as each jam began, the next five players on each side hit the track. Those who wanted to play the most learned quickly that the line of white shirts was usually shorter, and generally, if you were willing to jam, you could get a lot more reps in. You could be in a pack with some of the best players on the planet or in a mix-up of your committee members, or suddenly find yourself as the only person with any real experience on the track. One of my OHRD teammates, Quiet Storm, actually had her first scrimmage ever at the Las Vegas WFTDACon she attended, in her first year in roller derby. I believe she blocked in her first jam with four players who played at championships regularly, and I will never forget how exhilarated she looked coming off the track. The officials used the scrimmage as a training ground, trying out any recently ratified rules or teaching newer officials who might not have mentors locally the ins and outs of whistles and penalty tracking.

BrewCon was the third annual WFTDA meeting, so the meeting part was sparse in relation to some later years. There were probably only 100 reps total there, as there weren't even 100 leagues in WFTDA at the time. We met en masse at round tables in the hotel's conference center every morning, gulping down coffee to assuage hangovers before splitting off into separate tracks for officials, marketing, gameplay, membership, et cetera.

While this was my first go-around as a rep, I did have some experience working with some WFTDA folks. OHRD had stepped up to host the first Eastern Regional Playoff Tournament the year prior. Deemed Heartland Havoc, it spanned three days in August 2007 at the Greater Columbus Convention Center, with 12 teams from east of the Mississippi River, the top three of whom would go on to face off with the top three west of the Mississippi at Nationals in Austin later that autumn. We'd done double duty, playing in the tournament and hosting it as well. And at the 11th hour, when a men's focused cable channel (the now defunct Mav TV) contacted the WFTDA to film the event for later broadcast, I ended up coordinating with WFTDA for last minute needs like space to hold interviews and film the quick shots that would lead in to commercials. This is how I ended up with a WFTDA job before the end of day one of BrewCon, before Ziggy had even arrived in Milwaukee. And yes, she laughed about this when I told her that evening.

Basically, since I already knew some marketing folks, I went to the marketing meetings, and when no one offered to volunteer for the job of archiving press coverage, I casually raised my hand. At the time, I thought I was taking on a tiny job of little consequence; and ultimately, that was true. But within a year, I moved on to a different position in the membership committee, heading up the curriculum for the apprentice program to take in new leagues and show them the WFTDA ropes. Then over the next few years, I would be nominated to serve as the membership committee chair, and then membership pillar officer, before being elected to the board as vice president in 2015. Yada, yada, yada.

The officers in WFTDA are responsible for overseeing pillars of the organization: membership, games, officiating, marketing, regulatory, and technology. While they are volunteers, they are also running a lot of the day-to-day business of the organization. Most pillars also have a staff person now. The officers, the staff, and the board of directors all work fairly closely together—as closely as is possible when they are literally located all over the world. We met annually in person as a larger group for a retreat, usually in January, and we had monthly calls for our subgroups. As membership officer I was responsible mostly for managing our large volunteer pool, tracking leagues as they joined WFTDA, and making sure they contributed to the org (with volunteer hours, votes, and dues). I also got the opportunity to participate in the larger conversations as part of all my leadership roles.

Many roller derby leagues are nonprofit organizations, including the WFTDA, which is a 501(c)3, an IRS categorization that makes you tax exempt but requires you meet certain criteria to remain so. Because so many of our organizations were founded by people without a lot of experience in nonprofit management, and because ours was a culture of information sharing, there were sometimes things that were accepted as truth that weren't entirely accurate. One of these things was whether a tax-exempt nonprofit could be "political."

We'd always had the blanket idea that anything related to political issues was off the table. But as we became a more sophisticated organization, and as we reckoned with the ways that our larger society affected WFTDA, our member leagues, our players, and our officials, we were struggling with how to balance this. Once we had staff with more savvy, we began to realize that it wasn't that we couldn't take a political stand at all; we had to do so in a way that meshed with IRS regulations. And those specifically stipulate that 501(c)3s cannot participate in political campaigns and cannot have lobbying be their primary activity. Easy enough.

The tagline WFTDA has used on marketing materials for a long time is "Real. Strong. Athletic. Revolutionary." Once we realized the great deal of leeway we had within those IRS restrictions, we knew we could live up to that last word—revolutionary—in a whole new way, displaying the values we held so dear within our sport to the outside world. We could proclaim what roller derby was, not just as a sport, but as a community.

Some of that had already been happening as we got press coverage of our policies regarding transgender athletes in our sport. WFTDA had made an early attempt at writing an inclusionary policy but had missed the mark by including the possibility of needing to submit hormone tests, much like the problematic International Olympic Committee policies. After protest from some of our member leagues, the policy was rewritten as a statement of inclusion. Any mention of hormone levels was removed and the statement essentially boils down to "If you think this is where you belong and are comfortable here, then you do belong here."

This statement also means the organization now has conversations with vendors when we host a tournament in any city. WFTDA asks for at least one gender-neutral restroom facility and tries to prep vendors that our community may not look like what they expect or are used to but our expectation is that all members of our community will be treated with respect. And when some states passed anti-trans ballot measures and laws, it prompted conversation among our membership about whether WFTDA would host events there—whether it's better to boycott or to go ahead and host and educate, as well as support our member league who is dealing with this discrimination at a local level.

The first major statement I remember us releasing while I was on the board was in direct response to a policy that then president Donald Trump had put into effect, the so-called Muslim ban. The executive order that prohibited citizens of seven countries from entering the US was signed in late January 2017. It was racist, xenophobic, and motivated by religious hate under the flimsy disguise of protecting national security. And it immediately began to have an effect on roller derby.

While none of the seven countries listed in the ban had WFTDA member teams, there were citizens of those countries—and refugees from them—playing for teams all over the world. Several Swedish teams had members who might not be able to travel to the US for tournaments their teams had planned to participate in the following month, and as a result, their teams were considering not making the trip at all. The political situation in the US was quickly making roller derby players from other locales wonder if travel to the US was safe for them. And with all the 2017 postseason tournaments having been scheduled in US locations, except one playoff in Malmö, Sweden, feeling safe traveling to the US was crucial.

So those of us in WFTDA leadership drafted a statement to release. It was succinct—a mere four sentences:

> The Women's Flat Track Derby Association stands in solidarity against the United States' discriminatory executive order which issued immigration restrictions regarding lawful immigrants, nonimmigrants, and refugees from Iraq, Syria, Sudan, Iran, Somalia, Libya and Yemen. We believe the diversity of our member leagues, volunteers, staff and worldwide community makes our organization stronger, and we are committed to inclusive and anti-discrimination practices. As an international organization, free and open travel is vital to our community. As the states of Minnesota and Washington actively tackle this issue, we lend our collective voice to their movement in opposition of this executive order and support efforts to overturn it.

It may not have had a major effect. It almost certainly never reached the eyes of anyone in the US administration. But it did get some press coverage, which prompted a conversation about the "unintended consequences" of such a ban, and particularly the outsize effects on sporting competitions. And perhaps a bigger deal to our organization in the long term, it set up the possibility—and the expectation—that we would take a stand on issues that affected our organization and our members. And it reminded those members who were directly affected that we all try to understand what each of us is going through, and we try to have each other's backs.

10 Racism in Roller Derby

Derby people prefer to stay busy. Over social media, I've watched and learned as my teammates develop new hobbies and interests during our forced break from our beloved sport. Blitz Lemon has begun collecting and selling antiques, and is taking a welding class. Betty and BrutaChris and Avocado Tocstop and Chic'n Scratch and countless others have started shredding skate parks and bowls and any slab of city concrete they come across. Shayna Scully has a new obsession with shrooms, which thrive in the wet, hot, dark spots of Ohio. Scully has taught me about mycelium, the branching, interconnected network below the ground, transferring nutrients and enzymes and information, absorbing rot and pushing mushrooms up through the soil or bark like gorgeous, unexpected fruit.

Many of us have taken up protesting as our new hobby.

Roller derby people are interesting people. We are full up on outcasts and queers and punk rock aestheticists, the more outwardly obvious of our ilk. But we also include lifelong jocks, loners looking for a way in, folks of every walk of life and occupation and hobby and political affiliation, a wide array of identities. And we are, as a whole, extremely White.

In my time playing roller derby with two separate leagues, I have skated with four Black skaters total. This is not only unacceptable, but inexplicable. The history of Black roller skating in America is decades long. Unsurprisingly, it is also wholly informed by the racism of this country and this country's lingering segregations.

In the 1960s, during the civil rights movement, Black Americans found refuge in Black skate night at roller rinks. The segregated evenings were coded as "MLK Night" or "Soul Night" or "Gospel Night," and though the name has sometimes changed, the circumstances haven't much; today, those "Adult" or "Top 40" nights—say, those I attend here in Columbus at the United Skates of America—are the last vestiges of Black skate nights at the local rink. The Black history of skating has finally gained a higher profile in recent years. A 2018 HBO doc titled *United Skates* connects Black roller skating's past to present and amplifies the impact of Black skating subculture, the connections between it and music groups like Salt-N-Pepa, Queen Latifah, and N.W.A., and the continued threat of closure Black-frequented or Black-owned rinks face today.

During the pandemic, every White girl and her mom started buying skates, started filming retro-filtered Tik Toks and Instagrams. In response, social media users flooded platforms with informational memes about Black skate dancing and jam skating. The Daily Beast published "The Rich History of Black Roller Skating" in June 2020:

> Rinks were the site of many peaceful protests. One skater from Illinois named Reverend Koen speaks in the film about the KKK attacking picketers. The rink would later close. "They would rather die than integrate," he says.
>
> But determined Black skaters found a metaphor in their attempts to break down barriers at rinks: keep one foot in front of the other. "Forward forever and backwards never," Reverend Koen says.
>
> Ledger Smith, known as "Roller Man," skated 685 miles from Chicago to DC to attend the March on Washington, wearing a placard that read "FREEDOM" around his neck. He lost 10 pounds on the way and almost got run over by a racist driver in Fort Wayne, Indiana.

"He didn't do a single trick," Reggie told The Daily Beast. "He was just persistent. Skating outside, those legs start to hurt. But he was rolling with purpose."

When I attend Adult Night at one of two skate rinks in Columbus, the crowd is always predominantly Black. The skaters are always the most talented skaters I have ever seen. It makes no sense that roller derby is as White a sport as it is. Or, it makes perfect sense because accessibility, whether it be accessibility of time, money, exposure, knowledge, health care, health in general, is segregated. This country's systemic white supremacy is as quotidian as it is far-reaching, and throughout 2020 and 2021 we watched it play out on wheels, on the streets, in the pandemic, and on the steps of the Capitol.

And so some of us, we've been protesting the inequitable violence of these United States. We've been fighting for something better, wondering how long it will take US Americans to realize we are only as good as our fellow people, that when we hurt each other, we hurt ourselves. As the abolitionist Ruth Wilson Gilmore says, "Where life is precious, life is precious." We are supposed to be the mycelium, not the rot.

Pain Train is from Oklahoma. She is Black, she is tall, her style is glamour-punk-weirdo, she looks like a model for athletics or an athlete who moonlights as a model. She sweats as much as I do, and for this, I adore her. Pain Train's strength and talent and hard work and general excellence earned her a college basketball scholarship. Pain Train is easily one of the best roller derby players I have ever encountered—and I know I say that about a lot of my teammates, my loves, but I can't help it if it's true.

The thing about Pain Train is she is brilliant and she will not bullshit you. She will tell you what you do not want but need to hear. She is hilarious and kind and easily distracted and basically incredible at anything she tries. Right now, I'm going to bet Pain Train is wearing a faux fur coat, some slick burgundy Oxfords, tuxedo pants, glitter, and lipstick. Maybe she's popped in some canine fangs, if the occasion calls for it. She's probably making art or a podcast or a costume for the Renaissance festival. She may be doing all three at once. She's probably not sleeping enough because her brain never stops going.

Here is a list of things I have witnessed or know of secondhand, things that have happened to Pain Train via roller derby:

- Told she is "too aggressive," though her level of gameplay is never more so than anyone else's in this FULL-contact sport.
- More specifically, she once got a penalty and was told by the referee, "That was a legal hit but it was way too aggressive. Legal though. But too aggressive."
- In this very same game, a White player punched Pain Train in the throat. It was what you might call an aggressive move, and uhhh, definitely not a legal one. There was no discussion of aggression with this throat-punching player.
- A penalty is called by identifying the player's jersey color and number. At an away game, a penalty is called for Pain Train. The ref yells out, "Black! Double zero!" Our jerseys are white.
- One night, driving home from practice, Pain Train was pulled over by a cop. This happened before. It would happen again. The cop insisted the car might be stolen, though there was no proof, no report. The cop tugged on his gun, then demanded Pain Train get out of her truck.

Columbus police are corrupt. This may come across as a controversial opinion, but here are the facts. They've been (and are) under several federal investigations.[1] Drug cartel unit police have been caught redistributing fentanyl to the community, repeatedly. The Columbus Police

---

1   Here is one source of many: Elisha Fieldstadt, "Federal Judge Finds That Columbus Police Ran 'Amok' during Peaceful Protests, Restricts Uses of Force," NBC News, updated May 1, 2021, www.nbcnews.com.

Department has one of the highest numbers of fatal police shootings in the country. Most of the people CPD have fatally shot are Black. As of this writing, Columbus is tied with the NYPD for most children shot and killed by police, both departments only behind Chicago. In the last five years, CPD shot and killed five children, all of whom were Black, including 16-year-old Ma'Khia Bryant. Ma'Khia had called police for help from her Columbus foster home, minutes after the conviction of Derek Chauvin for his murder of George Floyd. Instead of helping Ma'Khia, who was being attacked by several adults, CPD showed up and shot her on sight.

CPD has been repeatedly investigated for excessive force. They are known for racial profiling, failures to train, failures to supervise, failures to discipline. Some of my teammates and I were protesting police brutality downtown when a Columbus police officer half a block away stomped and crushed the kneecap of another protester. The same police department will stand down and allow hundreds of White Ohio State University students to flip cars after a football game loss or win, but deploy teargas during a peaceful protest and crush kneecaps as a response to accusations of police brutality. Protesting their gross overreach, their constant abuses of power, became, in the last few years, less of a hobby for many of my teammates and more of a lifestyle.

This makes sense. Roller derby is collectivist. As a sport, as a league, we are skaters and officials and volunteers and coaches. We are not siloed, and leadership is fluid and many-armed. Our internal governance is the closest thing to actual democracy I've come across. We are all working toward one goal (when we're doing things right) because that's synchronicity. Or symbiosis. Or society. But society is racist, and roller derby, a reflection or microcosm of society, is racist too—in implicit and explicit ways. What good is our collectivism in the streets if we do not apply that same justice-seeking fervor to the track?

Pain Train says admitting our faults is the first step. Then White people have to make a real, constant, unyielding effort to change league culture. She says, "Leagues want to believe the few and far between Black skaters are a circumstantial thing, nothing to do with some reckoning of Whiteness and its impact on everyone else. Leagues full of *only* White people want to think that Black people, people of color, just didn't show up. Anti-racism is not a place you arrive at. You have to keep trying, you cannot fix one thing, you must address all. If you can open your eyes and accept those criticisms, you are already ahead of the game."

When I described the summer of 2020 to Pain Train, getting tear gassed by CPD for standing on a sidewalk and peacefully protesting, when I described the feeling of being there with my teammates, she laughed and offered a very Ohio perspective. "Ohio is my favorite team I've ever skated for. You guys are White and gay. I know that Ohio . . . if shit goes down, all of Ohio is going to jail. I would protest with Ohio. People on the team, the league . . . the introspection of this team is kinda radical. The willingness to look in. Ohio is gritty and basic, but in the best possible way. Ohio works. They don't brag on themselves, they just do it. Ohio just does shit."

Though that was gratifying to hear, we weren't always this way, and we *aren't* always this way. Pain Train motivated a huge portion of that introspective radicalism by being open about her perspective, by being brave and generous enough to share her experiences. When I told Pain Train I was afraid to mess up this chapter, she told me to be honest about the fact that I don't have all the answers or information, that I don't know everything, and that's okay. In fact, that's kind of the point: "Report from the recognition that you don't know everything, Kegel."

So: I don't have all the answers. I am a White lady, and the way I live and exist in the world is different from the way Pain Train lives and exists in the world. I know this better than many White people because my grandmother is Korean. I've watched her experience racism firsthand, I know the impact white supremacy has had on her life and my family. But I also know that even as I am ethnically Korean, the world sees me, a White lady, and reacts accordingly, as if Whiteness were naturally default or norm and not just a concept made up to justify rampant inhumanity. I know that racism is in roller derby as it is in the world at large, in this country, the Ohio of countries—the US of A. And I know the roller derby community as a whole has long been ignorant of, or worse, outright ignored, the problem of racism in roller derby.

I know that Pain Train knows all this intimately, in ways I could never fathom, would never ever encounter, and so I also know when it's time to shut up and listen.

Jordyn "Pain Train" Blanson
(Credit: Candace Moser Stafford)

OHIO PLAYER PROFILE: A WORD FROM PAIN TRAIN

So. It's this way:

Come here to roller derby and experience the same shit you experience every fucking day. We'll even let you (pay to) play, come and skate for us, and we'll let you, and that's enough.

Just skate. And go home.

It was late at night, after 9:30 p.m. Our practice ran late. Then I got on the road late because I was working in the truck on the company laptop, did some work before I got on the interstate.

I was living in Dayton and had to drive one hour and 20 minutes from Columbus to Dayton. I was in my new company vehicle, that bright orange tangelo truck, you know, gaudy and ostentatious. There was no one else on the road when I saw lights behind, nearing the end of Columbus city limits. You know, how you can see the skyline in the distance?

He pulls me over and asks, "Do you know why you got pulled over?"

No.

"Someone called you in as suspicious."

But there's no one around. How? This quickly? On the interstate?

"I'm just doing my job, you don't have to investigate, just give me your license and registration."

The vehicle is a company car. It has manufacturer plates, not standard. It says manufacturer on the plates and police know what that means. It's not unusual. The registration says this vehicle is registered under my company.

He says, "Do you have proof you're allowed to drive this vehicle?"

Um, it's a company car . . .

"Your name isn't attached to this vehicle."

Because it's a company car. It's registered to the company.

He says I have to prove it. "Don't you have some kind of name badge? Show me proof you can have this car."

I don't have a name badge, I'm a field employee—

"All those companies' employees have a name badge."

That's not true, I'm an employee and I don't have one.

"You should have a name badge."

But here's my laptop, I can show you my email. Here's a company sticker on my stuff. My phone. I can show you my email . . . I can show you that I work for this company.

"You can't prove this is your car."

I can show you I work for this company.

"I'm gonna need you to put your hands on the wheel."

For what?

"You can't prove this is your car. Put your hands on the wheel."

You are profiling me. I have other forms of identification. I have told you.

"PUT YOUR HANDS ON THE WHEEL!"

He pulls his gun just over the lip of the holster, making it clear he will shoot. I tell him to run it. Run the VIN. Run it. I run my mouth,

Oh you look big and bad but you're gonna call in the plates and feel like a fool when you find out this is my car.

He calls up the VIN to see if it's stolen. It's not.

I guffaw, I say, I expect an apology for you being so woefully obtuse (it's all adrenaline now).

You called it in as stolen and nothing was wrong.

Do you feel less threatened, do you feel more in control now? I was kinda out of my mind.

"Pretty much just don't do it again," he says.

What am I not doing again—getting profiled?

Then I realized how wild I was, running my mouth. He left. I called my mom, had a big, long cry when it hit me:

If I just disappeared.

If I hadn't come home . . . I live alone.

I work from home, my family isn't here, I'm not in my city, how long—

How long before they realized I was gone? I could disappear off the face of the earth.

And the media might say there was a reason, a justified reason for this cop . . .

It hit me. My mom was nervous. She called every time I came home from practice. When are you leaving/when are you coming back?

After the fact I realized I could have asked for his badge number. But in the moment I was just so pissed off my brain was . . .

More than anything else, I thought, what truth is there to share? If I died, disappeared, there is no truth.

Roller derby likes to think it's excluded from the negativity of the world. Like it's above it all, or outside.

And maybe there are gender/sexuality freedoms, maybe it's fine to be queer and trans and out, but . . . roller derby is not inclusive just because it's gay as hell.

It's just gay as hell.

Roller derby is a microcosm of society, it includes all that's out there. But it (roller derby) is more dangerous in some ways because this community believes it is beyond reproach.

Why is our space any safer than society? How? What do we do differently? I've asked people and they say, *My mindset is different.* Okay. But they can't say what they do, what practices they implement, to break away from a White-centered, patriarchal culture—and they don't have consciousness, they don't know.

Not everyone gets to *just go home.*

—Pain Train

A Word from Amy Spears: Roller Derby in the Future

"I can't. I have roller derby."

This phrase has been uttered by so many players, officials, and others involved in our sport that it's become cliché. It appears on T-shirts, on mugs, in memes. We say it to our friends, our families, folks involved in our other hobbies—if we have time to still have them. It's almost never a little white lie to get out of something you don't want to do, because it's so very true. We always have roller derby. Roller derby practice, derby meetings, promotional appearances, volunteering for community events. Maybe I have to skate in circles, doing stopping and hitting drills for two hours, maybe I need to meet to talk about how to pay off business debts or maybe I need to get to the rink to teach a troop of Girl Scouts to skate. In the latter example, I got paired with the dramatic child who would just release all her muscles when she felt she might fall down, yelling, "I can't!" and leaving me to catch her awkwardly and hold her up, *Weekend at Bernie's* style. My arms were quite sore, but she was a delight.

But for the past couple years, we didn't have roller derby.

The question looms as to what happens long term as we begin our comeback. Forty dollars a month for dues but no time commitment or requirement to volunteer was a small price to pay, relatively speaking, for a lot of us while things were shut down. But what about that plus adding the practice time? And eventually, the games, the setup, the marketing, the meetings. Oh, the meetings. We got awfully used to having our evenings free. To spending time on the couch with our dogs, our partners, and not having to jump up after shoving dinner down our throats to drive to the warehouse.

The training committee came back to all this earlier than most as we prepped and put out surveys. We asked, "Who wants to come back right now and feels safe doing so? Who would rather have an individual skate time slot? Do you live with a teammate or work with one? Tell us so that we can make a plan of attack to avoid transferring COVID among ourselves and stay on skates for good once we're back on them."

The production committee organized cleanup of the warehouse, which had been alternately described as looking like post-volcano Pompeii and like it was wearing a fleece blanket, the dust of the other tenants in the space having had 18 months to fly into our space and settle.

We dropped off our shop vacs and signed up for shifts to take turns slowly sucking up all the evidence of the disuse. It was an oddly satisfying thing to see the cracks emerge in the floor surface as the dust that filled them was pulled back out. Our masks did double duty, protecting our lungs from the virus and from the detritus.

A lot of people skated outdoors during the early days of the pandemic, and many of them picked up new skills on ramps and half-pipes rather than derby skills, but others hadn't had skates on their feet since March 2020. Most of us fell somewhere in between.

If a new rookie coming into roller derby might take a year or more to gain enough skill to jump into a B-team level game, how long would it take 60 skaters with varying degrees of derby skill and fitness after two years of pandemic lockdown life to get back up to speed? I've said a few times that this will be the great equalizer, the only time that new skaters can come in and have the veterans not be light years ahead, because even if someone never stopped working out (cough, cough, Bigg Rigg), never gained the pandemic 15, never lost their quad strength, they still haven't played roller derby for the longest continuous time since they started playing roller derby. When else will anyone be able to walk in the door and find that no one there has played roller derby in the past two years?

I have played our sport under every official rule set. I find myself forgetting what is still a rule and what may have changed. There were tweaks to scoring in the season before we shut down that didn't have time to permanently imprint on my brain. I am not sure I understand how to play—let alone win—at roller derby anymore. The most relevance roller derby rules have had for me in recent history was when my team at work had to socially distance 400 classrooms at OSU. I could set stickers out at six-foot intervals without measuring because of all my experience judging distances in my head to be in compliance with the rules of pack definition. It's a tiny bit easier without wheels on your feet.

We'll get there. I know we will. But I don't foresee being back in a lot of circumstances from my own derby history—perhaps ever again. I just turned 46 years old. Even if I hold it together to play until I'm 50, the idea of traveling to a tournament with teams from Europe, South America, Australia seems unlikely to be a reasonable expectation. It's just going to be different. And we're going to have to be okay with that.

We knew it would probably be months before we would be able to scrimmage again. And that we'll probably play games among ourselves before facing off against nearby teams.

Finally, hopefully, someday the situation in the world will allow us to venture out into the kinds of activities we were used to before the pandemic: games, international travel, and venues filled with spectators. I still get nervous in a store when someone stands too close to me, and attending my nephew's outdoor baseball game was more people than I'd been around in almost two years, so the thought of that is both anxiety producing and exciting. It sounds nearly impossible right now that we should be able to return to what once was—and ultimately, hopefully, we won't return to exactly as we were before, but to something far better.

It can be better too. It will be better. We all got a good wake-up call about a number of things in the past few years—the effect of huge time commitments on our mental health, prioritizing what really matters, issues of racial equity in our entire sport from local to international levels. If we do this right, when we come back we will address these things and not step back into our old ways because "that's how we've always done it." We have an opportunity to use a critical lens and change our sport for the better, because if nothing else, the pandemic gave us a forced thousand-mile overview of how we've been operating.

Epilogue

In the Ohio winter, we skate without heat; in summer, we nearly
die from it. The southside of Columbus, once an industrial epi-
center of steel and glass, is crowded with overgrown tarmac, fenced-
off lots of semis and construction materials, a hoard of dilapidated
warehouses. Ours is cordoned off into several functioning sections
of labor. Half of it buzzes 24/7: men with buzzing saws, forklifts, and
the occasional sounds of Jethro Tull or Journey pierce the barriers of
insulation doing their best to imitate walls. We, too, do our best to
stop each other, using only our bodies. We roll into, away, back again,
as heat and dust and likely a bit of asbestos seep through to our half
of the warehouse.

Whistles and penalty calls echo through the cavern of concrete,
our space further divided by a wonky line of office cubicle panels. The
brick wall opposite the office cubicles is lovingly and/or laughably
padded with blue gymnasium mats, a harking back to gym class, to
more youthful moments of physical humiliation. We map a track on
the cracked concrete with hot pink or mustard tape, and we retape
the oval several times a season. The tape is sturdy but cannot with-
stand skates and toe stops or the unknown liquid oozing up through
the floor as the freezing temps end, as the concrete releases humidity
and expands.

Sometimes, if the air is particularly polluted, we wear bandannas
over our mouths. We upgraded to masks in the case of unending pandemic. Sometimes we skate in parkas and gloves, and sometimes we
skate in bras and underwear, and most any time we wear loud, festive
socks. Our shared half of the warehouse is poorly lit, one side stacked
with old hospital equipment and metal shelves of junk someone must
be trying to salvage and sell on eBay.

On the other side, we practice three late nights a week. We play a '90s hip-hop playlist and we skate, we hit, we stretch, we fly. We sweat and weep and laugh. We keep practicing and we don't stop. A whistle blows, we go all hands in.

Ohio 'til we die.

Acknowledgments

Samantha

Big thanks to Samara Rafert. This was her idea!

The team at Swallow Press and Ohio University Press let me and Amy play, and we cannot thank them enough for that.

Ohio Roller Derby—my dreammates, volunteers, officials, league members—I am forever grateful to have them all in my life. Let's all get more tattoos. Amy Spears is my forever Captain and made this whole book thing fun. Really, truly, fun. We're a good team.

Samantha "Kegel Scout" Tucker
(Credit: Candace Moser Stafford)

I am lucky for the enduring support of my agent, Katie Kotchman. She waits ever so patiently. There's no one else I'd rather make things for/with.

Many thanks to my professors at Colorado State: Sue Doe, E. J. Levy, DBQ, and Debby Thompson; to Stephanie G'Schwind, editor-in-chief of *Colorado Review* and best mentor ever; and to my CSU lovelies: Meg, Amanda, Lydia, Vani, and Whitney, the most important teachers I've ever had. Thank you to Casey and Bryan Mirick for feeding my stomach, soul, butt, et cetera.

Thanks to the faculty and staff of the OSU English department, who gave me Ohio: Kathy, Lee, Michelle, Tammy. My MFA classmates taught me much, but no one more than my nonfiction cohort, and especially Sonya, Jacinta, Dylan, Jessie, Kim, and Michael.

The invaluable generosity of the Ohio Arts Council and the Vermont Studio Center allowed and encouraged me to create art.

I love my family, who made me. I'm including the Tuckers, Santos, Arnolds, Lemmings, Kerleys, and Nostadt-Hermans. Janine, Lee, and Heather, who always keep me grounded and remind me where we're from, where we're headed. None of this happened without Jesse, and for this I'm grateful and proud. I love you. We are family for life. And Buster and Meryl can't read this, but they are the best and I adore them. They take care of us.

Finally, to Megan, who believes, who cheers me on, who endlessly gives: thank you for helping me be who I am. Thank you for being you. I love you, I love you, I love you.

Amy Spears
(Credit: Candace Moser Stafford)

Amy

Every single person w
a part of Ohio Roller
point in history, in any
uted to this book, wheth
mentioned or not. Than
ing this story and contin
and making this the plac
to be for the past decad
Special thanks to Scarlet
took that crucial first step

Kegel, you're a team
many more ways after t
you better carry on long af
has given out on me. Tha
letting me give up on this

To my other derby family, my WFTDA friends, the gre
group of type-A people dedicated to a niche cause who ever e
sometimes, the only people who can possibly understand—I
you enough for all we've worked through.

To all my friends who have come to see me skate in wh
I happen to be in, thank you for sticking by me through th
consuming adventure and understanding when I can only h
10 minutes in between games.

Thanks to my family supporting me and only occasional
back on whatever harebrained scheme I've started as of lat
judging this bizarro world you've been plunged into when yo
watch me play and not blinking when I utter phrases like "I
on a loan for a skate floor." Maya and Evan, go find your ro
and do it.

And finally, to all those roller derby folks all over the pla
haven't met yet, I know you've got these stories too. Keep it u
the world.

Acknowledgments

Samantha

Big thanks to Samara Rafert. This was her idea!

The team at Swallow Press and Ohio University Press let me and Amy play, and we cannot thank them enough for that.

Ohio Roller Derby—my dream-mates, volunteers, officials, league members—I am forever grateful to have them all in my life. Let's all get more tattoos. Amy Spears is my forever Captain and made this whole book thing fun. Really, truly, fun. We're a good team.

I am lucky for the enduring sup-

Samantha "Kegel Scout" Tucker
(Credit: Candace Moser Stafford)

port of my agent, Katie Kotchman. She waits ever so patiently. There's no one else I'd rather make things for/with.

Many thanks to my professors at Colorado State: Sue Doe, E. J. Levy, DBQ, and Debby Thompson; to Stephanie G'Schwind, editor-in-chief of *Colorado Review* and best mentor ever; and to my CSU lovelies: Meg, Amanda, Lydia, Vani, and Whitney, the most important teachers I've ever had. Thank you to Casey and Bryan Mirick for feeding my stomach, soul, butt, et cetera.

Thanks to the faculty and staff of the OSU English department, who gave me Ohio: Kathy, Lee, Michelle, Tammy. My MFA classmates taught me much, but no one more than my nonfiction cohort, and especially Sonya, Jacinta, Dylan, Jessie, Kim, and Michael.

The invaluable generosity of the Ohio Arts Council and the Vermont Studio Center allowed and encouraged me to create art.

I love my family, who made me. I'm including the Tuckers, Santos, Arnolds, Lemmings, Kerleys, and Nostadt-Hermans. Janine, Lee, and Heather, who always keep me grounded and remind me where we're from, where we're headed. None of this happened without Jesse, and for this I'm grateful and proud. I love you. We are family for life. And Buster and Meryl can't read this, but they are the best and I adore them. They take care of us.

Finally, to Megan, who believes, who cheers me on, who endlessly gives: thank you for helping me be who I am. Thank you for being you. I love you, I love you, I love you.

Amy Spears
(Credit: Candace Moser Stafford)

Amy

Every single person who has been a part of Ohio Roller Derby at any point in history, in any role, contributed to this book, whether specifically mentioned or not. Thank you for living this story and continuing to do so and making this the place I've wanted to be for the past decade and a half. Special thanks to Scarlette Fury, who took that crucial first step.

Kegel, you're a teammate in so many more ways after this project; you better carry on long after my body has given out on me. Thanks for not letting me give up on this wacky idea.

To my other derby family, my WFTDA friends, the greatest ragtag group of type-A people dedicated to a niche cause who ever existed—and sometimes, the only people who can possibly understand—I can't thank you enough for all we've worked through.

To all my friends who have come to see me skate in whatever city I happen to be in, thank you for sticking by me through this wild, all-consuming adventure and understanding when I can only hang out for 10 minutes in between games.

Thanks to my family supporting me and only occasionally pushing back on whatever harebrained scheme I've started as of late. For not judging this bizarro world you've been plunged into when you come to watch me play and not blinking when I utter phrases like "I cosigned on a loan for a skate floor." Maya and Evan, go find your roller derby and do it.

And finally, to all those roller derby folks all over the planet who I haven't met yet, I know you've got these stories too. Keep it up and tell the world.